Microsoft® Office Access™ 2007

Level 3 (Second Edition)

Microsoft® Office Access™ 2007: Level 3 (Second Edition)

Part Number: 084889
Course Edition: 1.0

NOTICES

HELP US IMPROVE OUR COURSEWARE

Microsoft® Office Access™ 2007: Level 3 (Second Edition)

Lesson 5: Making Reports More Effective

Lesson 6: Maintaining an Access Database

About This Course

Your training in and use of Microsoft® Office Access™ 2007 has provided you with a solid foundation in the basic and intermediate skills of working in Microsoft® Office Access™ 2007. You have worked with the various Access objects, such as tables, queries, forms, and reports. In this course, you will extend your knowledge into some of the more specialized and advanced capabilities of Access by structuring existing data, writing advanced queries, working with macros, enhancing forms and reports, and maintaining a database.

Your basic knowledge of Microsoft® Office Access™ 2007 to this point allows you to create simple, functional databases. By further exploring Microsoft® Office Access™ 2007's advanced features, you will be able to work on a simple database and turn it into a robust, highly functional one. The results will not only be a joy for users to work with, but they will make your job much easier.

Course Description

Target Student

This course is for the individual whose job responsibilities include working with related tables; creating advanced queries, forms, and reports; writing macros to automate common tasks; and performing general database maintenance. It is also designed as one in a series of courses for students pursuing the Microsoft® Office Specialist Certification for Microsoft® Office Access™ 2007, and it is a prerequisite to take more advanced courses in Microsoft® Office Access™ 2007.

Course Prerequisites

To ensure your success, knowledge of basic and intermediate features of Access tables, relationships, and queries, forms, and reports is recommended. The following Element K courses or equivalent knowledge are recommended:

- *Microsoft® Office Access™ 2007: Level 1*
- *Microsoft® Office Access™ 2007: Level 2*

How to Use This Book

As a Learning Guide

Each lesson covers one broad topic or a set of related topics. Lessons are arranged in order of increasing proficiency with *Microsoft® Access™ 2007*; skills you acquire in one lesson are used and developed in subsequent lessons. For this reason, you should work through the lessons in sequence.

We organized each lesson into results-oriented topics. Topics include all the relevant and supporting information you need to master *Microsoft® Access™ 2007*, and activities allow you to apply this information to practical hands-on examples.

You get to try out each new skill on a specially prepared sample file. This saves you typing time and allows you to concentrate on the skill at hand. Through the use of sample files, hands-on activities, illustrations that give you feedback at crucial steps, and supporting background information, this book provides you with the foundation and structure to learn *Microsoft® Access™ 2007* quickly and easily.

As a Review Tool

Any method of instruction is only as effective as the time and effort you are willing to invest in it. In addition, some of the information that you learn in class may not be important to you immediately, but it may become important later on. For this reason, we encourage you to spend some time reviewing the topics and activities after the course. For an additional challenge when reviewing activities, try the "What You Do" column before looking at the "How You Do It" column.

As a Reference

The organization and layout of the book makes it easy to use as a learning tool and as an after-class reference. You can use this book as a first source for definitions of terms, background information on given topics, and summaries of procedures.

Course Icons

Icon	Description
	A **Caution Note** makes students aware of potential negative consequences of an action, setting, or decision that are not easily known.
	Display Slide provides a prompt to the instructor to display a specific slide. Display Slides are included in the Instructor Guide only.
	An **Instructor Note** is a comment to the instructor regarding delivery, classroom strategy, classroom tools, exceptions, and other special considerations. Instructor Notes are included in the Instructor Guide only.
	Notes Page indicates a page that has been left intentionally blank for students to write on.
	A **Student Note** provide additional information, guidance, or hints about a topic or task.
	A **Version Note** indicates information necessary for a specific version of software.

Certification

This course is designed to help you prepare for the following certification.

Certification Path: Microsoft Certified Application Specialist: Microsoft® Access™ 2007

This course is one of a series of Element K courseware titles that addresses Microsoft Certified Application Specialist (MCAS) skill sets. The MCAS program is for individuals who use Microsoft's business desktop software and who seek recognition for their expertise with specific Microsoft products. Certification candidates must pass one or more product proficiency exams in order to earn Office Specialist certification.

Course Objectives

In this course, you will create complex Access databases by structuring existing data, writing advanced queries, working with macros, making effective use of forms and reports, and performing database maintenance.

You will:

- restructure data into appropriate tables to ensure data dependency and minimize redundancy.
- write advanced queries to analyze and summarize data.
- create and revise Microsoft® Office Access™ 2007 macros.
- display data more effectively in a form.
- customize reports by using various Microsoft® Office Access™ 2007 features, making them more effective.
- maintain your database using tools provided by Microsoft® Office Access™ 2007.

Course Requirements

Hardware

For this course, you will need one computer for each student and one for the instructor. Each computer will need the following minimum hardware components:

- A 1 GHz Pentium-class processor or faster.
- A minimum of 256 MB of RAM, with 512 MB of RAM recommended.
- A 10 GB hard disk or larger. You should have at least 1 GB of free hard disk space available for the Office installation.
- A CD-ROM drive.
- A mouse or other pointing device.
- A 1024 x 768 resolution monitor is recommended.
- Network cards and cabling for local network access.
- Internet access (contact your local network administrator).
- A printer (optional) or an installed printer driver. (Printers are not required; however, each PC must have an installed printer driver to use Print Preview.)
- A projection system to display the instructor's computer screen.

Software

- Microsoft® Office Professional Edition 2007
- Windows XP Professional with Service Pack 2
- Snapshot Viewer

Class Setup

Initial Class Setup

For initial class setup:

1. Install Windows XP Professional on an empty partition.
   - Leave the Administrator password blank.
   - For all other installation parameters, use values that are appropriate for your environment. (See your local network administrator if you need details.)

2. In Windows XP Professional, disable the Welcome screen. (This step ensures that students will be able to log on as the Administrator user regardless of other user accounts existing on the computer.) Click Start and choose Control Panel→User Accounts. Click Change The Way Users Log On And Off. Uncheck Use Welcome Screen. Click Apply Options.

3. On Windows XP Professional, install Service Pack 2. Use the Service Pack installation defaults.

4. For Windows XP Professional, click Start and choose Printers And Faxes. Under Printer Tasks, click Add A Printer and follow the prompts.

5. Run the Internet Connection Wizard to set up the Internet connection as appropriate for your environment if you did not do so during installation.

6. Log on to the computer as the Administrator user if you have not already done so.

7. Perform a complete installation, accepting all defaults, of Microsoft Office Professional 2007.

8. Minimize the Language Bar if it appears.

9. Display known file type extensions.

    a. Open Windows Explorer (right-click the Start button and then choose Explore).

    b. Choose Tools→Folder Options.

    c. On the View tab, in the Advanced Settings list box, uncheck Hide Extensions For Known File Types.

    d. Click Apply and then click OK.

    e. Close Windows Explorer.

10. On the course CD-ROM, open the 084_889 folder. Then, open the Data folder. Run the 084889dd.exe self-extracting file located in it. This will install a folder named 084889Data on your C drive. This folder contains all the data files that you will use to complete this course.

    Within each lesson folder, you may find a Solution folder. This folder contains solution files for the lesson's activities and lesson lab, which can be used by students to check their end results.

 The Production version of Microsoft® Office Professional 2007 has been used to perform this course setup.

Customize the Windows Desktop

Customize the Windows desktop to display the My Computer and My Network Places icons on the student and instructor systems by following these steps:

1. Right-click the desktop and choose Properties.

2. Select the Desktop tab.

3. Click Customize Desktop.

4. In the Desktop Items dialog box, check My Computer and My Network Places.

5. Click OK and click Apply.

6. Close the Display Properties dialog box.

Configure Trust Center Settings

1. From the Office Button menu, click the Access Options button.
2. Select the Trust Center category.
3. Click the Trust Center Settings button.
4. In the Trust Center dialog box, select the Macro Settings category and select the Enable All Macros option.
5. In the Trust Center dialog box, select the Trusted Locations category and click the Add New Location button.
6. In the Microsoft Office Trusted Location dialog box, click the Browse button and navigate to the C:\084889Data folder and click OK.
7. Check the Subfolders Of This Location Are Also Trusted check box.
8. In the Microsoft Office Trusted Location dialog box, click OK.
9. Click OK to close the Trust Center dialog box.
10. Click OK to close the Access Options dialog box.

Install Snapshot Viewer

1. From the **www.microsoft.com** website, download the Snapshot Viewer program.
2. Execute the snpvw.exe file to install Snapshot Viewer on your system. Accept the default values in the Snapshot Viewer Setup program.

Before Every Class

1. Log on to the computer as the Administrator user.
2. Delete any existing data files from the C:\084889Data folder.
3. Extract a fresh copy of the course data files from the CD-ROM provided with the course manual.

List of Additional Files

Printed with each activity is a list of files students open to complete that activity. Many activities also require additional files that students do not open, but are needed to support the file(s) students are working with. These supporting files are included with the student data files on the course CD-ROM or data disk. Do not delete these files.

1 | Structuring Existing Data

Lesson Time: 1 hour(s)

Lesson Objectives:

In this lesson, you will restructure data into appropriate tables to ensure data dependency and minimize redundancy.

You will:

● Restructure existing data using the Table Analyzer Wizard.

● Create a junction table to minimize redundant data.

● Modify the structure of tables to meet a change in target specification.

Introduction

You have worked with database objects in Microsoft® Office Access™ 2007. As an advanced-level user, you may have to improve databases that a beginner created. Or, you may need to inherit data originally stored in a different data format and figure out how to implement that data into Access. In this lesson, you will structure existing data.

Being able to identify and resolve problems with the design of tables will assist you in troubleshooting databases. Knowing the most efficient way to get existing data into well-designed Access tables will minimize data redundancy and save time in data entry.

TOPIC A
Analyze Tables

In Access, you have created tables from scratch and by using a wizard, but, in those cases, you did not have existing data to deal with. Consider a situation where you have improperly designed tables that already have data in them. You need to analyze and structure the data in these tables to create new tables that follow normalization standards. In this topic, you will analyze tables using the Table Analyzer Wizard.

If you need to create a new table structure, moving data from an existing table to new tables can be a tedious task. If you use the Table Analyzer Wizard to create new tables, the Analyzer will move the existing data for you. This saves you time because you do not have to write queries or transfer data from the old tables to the new ones.

First Normal Form

Definition:

First normal form (1NF) is a normal form that is used to design a table in which the value in each cell corresponds to its field name. It is the lowest normal form that ensures that a table contains only related data and each cell has a single value. It eliminates duplicate records by identifying a column or set of columns as a primary key.

Example:

In this Employee table, EmployeeID is the primary key. Before normalization, the EmployeeName field has two values, which consist of the first name and the last name of the employee. After applying first normal form, the EmployeeName field is split into EmployeeFirstName and EmployeeLastName fields that have one value each. Similarly, the City field is split into City and Country fields.

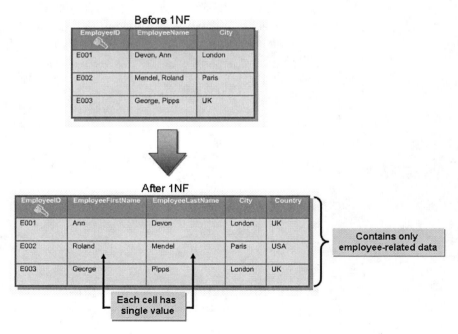

Second Normal Form

Definition:

Second normal form (2NF) is a normal form that is used to establish *functional dependency* in a table. A table that needs to conform to the second normal form should first satisfy the first normal form. It should also contain fields that are functionally dependent fully on the primary key field and not just part of the key. If any of the fields in the table are dependent on part of the primary key, then those fields are moved out to form another table. In this form, any inserting, updating, or deleting of data should not lead to any inconsistencies in the table.

Example:

In this Employee table, the primary key fields are EmployeeID and ProjectCode. Before normalization, the Hours field is dependant on both the primary key fields, but the Department field is dependant only on the EmployeeID primary key field. Based on the second normalization form, the Department field, which is not fully dependant on both the primary key fields, is moved to a new table.

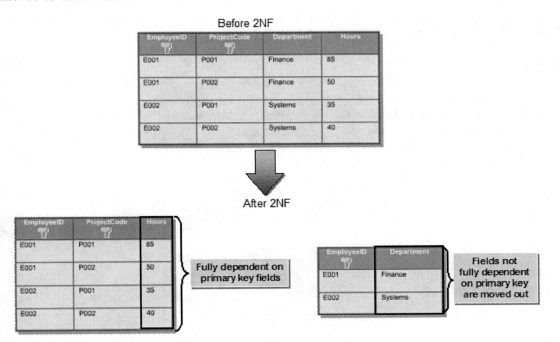

Functional Dependency

Functional dependency is established in a table when all the non-key fields are dependent only on the primary key field(s) of the table. For example, consider an Employee table with EmployeeID as the primary key field and EmployeeName and City as the non-key fields. Here, each EmployeeID will have a unique value. The EmployeeName and City fields are functionally dependent on the EmployeeID field because their values are solely determined by the entity represented by the EmployeeID and only the EmployeeID.

EmployeeID	EmployeeName	City
E001	Devon	London
E002	Ann	London
E003	Devon	London

Figure 1-1: *A table showing functional dependency.*

Third Normal Form

Definition:

Third normal form (3NF) is a normal form that is used to establish a *non-transitive dependency* in a table. A table that needs to conform to the third normal form should first satisfy the first and second normal forms. The third normal form ensures that the non-key fields do not depend on other non-key fields in the table. If a field in the table is dependent on a field other than the primary key field, then it is moved to a new table.

Example:

In this Employee table, the EmployeeID field is the primary key. Before normalization, the non-key fields Department and DeptHead are dependant on the primary key field. But the DeptHead field is also dependant on the Department field. Based on the third normal form that a non-key field should not be dependant on another non-key field, the DeptHead field is moved to a new table with the Department field. Thus, every employee can belong to only one department and every department can have only one department head.

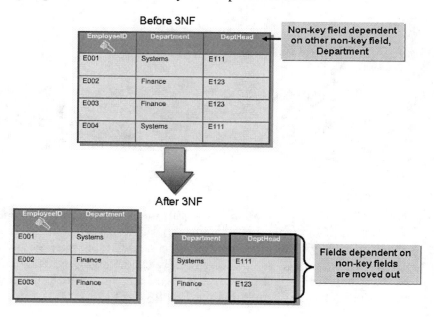

Transitive Dependency

Transitive dependency is established when a non-key field in a table is dependent on the primary key field as well as another non-key field. For example, consider an Employee table that has EmployeeID as the primary key field and Department and DeptHead as the other non-key fields. In this table, an employee can only belong to one Department; therefore, the Department field is functionally dependent on EmployeeID. An employee can have only one

DeptHead; therefore, DeptHead is also functionally dependent on EmployeeID. However, DeptHead is also dependent on Department because DeptHead will have unique values only when associated with the Department field. Here, DeptHead is dependent on the primary key field as well as another non-key field. This indicates transitive dependency. Therefore, according to 3NF, the Department and DeptHead fields will form a new table and the Department field will also be part of the original table.

EmployeeID	Department	DeptHead
E001	Systems	E111
E002	Finance	E123
E003	Finance	E123
E004	Systems	E111

Figure 1-2: *A table showing transitive dependency.*

The Table Analyzer Wizard

The *Table Analyzer Wizard* will help you manage existing Access data. The wizard will examine an existing database and make suggestions as to how to make the database run more efficiently. If you accept the suggestions given by the wizard, it will split the database into many tables according to the normalization rules. The wizard also sets the primary key for each new table. The wizard has an option that you can use to create a query to retrieve data from the original tables.

How to Analyze Tables

Procedure Reference: Restructure Table Data Using the Table Analyzer Wizard

To restructure table data using the Table Analyzer Wizard:

1. Open the database containing the table you want to analyze.
2. On the Database Tools tab, in the Analyze group, click Analyze Table to launch the Table Analyzer Wizard.
3. In the Table Analyzer Wizard, on the first page, observe the message explaining the problems caused by repeating information. Click Next.
4. Observe that the next page explains how Access will solve the problem. Click Next.
5. From the Tables list box, select the table you want the wizard to analyze. Click Next.
6. On the fourth page, select an option.
    *   Select the Yes, Let The Wizard Decide option in order to let the wizard analyze the table and split the database.
    *   Select the No, I Want To Decide option in order to manually analyze the table and split the database.
7. Click Next.
8. If necessary, split the tables, group the fields in the tables, and rename the tables. Click Next.
9. If necessary, in the Table Analyzer Wizard dialog box, click OK.
10. Confirm the primary keys or set new keys. Click Next.

11. Correct the typographical errors.
    - In the Correction column, correct the typographical errors.
    - Or, in case of no corrections, select the Leave As Is option.
12. Click Next.
13. If necessary, select the Yes, Create The Query option to create a query that has data from the original tables.
14. Click Finish.
15. Open the tables and verify that they are structured and follow normalization standards.

ACTIVITY 1-1

Analyzing Tables by Running the Table Analyzer Wizard

Data Files:

Structure.accdb

Before You Begin:

1. From the C:\084889Data\Structuring Existing Data folder, open the Structure.accdb database.

2. If necessary, in the Access Options dialog box, in the Current Database category, change the Document Window Options to Overlapping Windows.

3. Exit Access and open the structure.accdb database again.

Scenario:

You are an information analyst with a company. You have just joined the company and part of your new job is to provide support to Access users and help ensure the integrity of the data being used throughout the company. The sales manager asks you to review the table he has been using to track orders because he knows it contains redundant data. In an effort to save time, you have decided to try using the Table Analyzer Wizard to redesign the table and move the existing data.

What You Do	How You Do It
1. **Observe the records in the LonePineSales table.**	a. In the structure.accdb database, **open the LonePineSales table.**
	b. Observe the records in the table.
	c. **Close the table.**

2. **What can be the major problems with the data caused by a poor table design in the LonePineSales table?**

    a) Customer names and categories are repeated.

    b) The table contains fields that have no related data.

    c) There are no primary key fields assigned.

    d) The Category and Product fields cannot be kept in one table.

3. Run the Table Analyzer Wizard to the point where the data has been grouped into tables.

a. On the Ribbon, **select the Database Tools tab.**

b. In the Analyze group, **click Analyze Table** to launch the Table Analyzer Wizard.

 You need to remove the read-only attribute on a file to run the Table Analyzer Wizard.

c. In the Table Analyzer Wizard, in the The Table Analyzer: Looking At The Problem section, observe the message that lists the disadvantages of duplicating information in a table.

d. **Click Next.**

e. In the The Table Analyzer: Solving The Problem section, observe the suggested solution. It involves splitting the table so that the resultant tables are in first normal form.

f. **Click Next.**

g. In the Tables list box, **verify that LonePineSales is selected and click Next.**

h. **Verify that the Yes, Let The Wizard Decide option is selected and click Next** to split the table so that the resultant tables satisfy first normal form.

i. If necessary, **drag the title bars of the tables so that they are visible all at once.**

j. Observe the results.

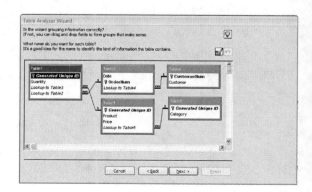

4. Rename the tables.

a. In the Table Analyzer Wizard, **verify that Table1 is selected.**

b. **Click the Rename Table button.**

c. In the Table Analyzer Wizard dialog box, **type *tblOrderDetails* and click OK** to rename the table.

d. **Rename the remaining tables with the following names:**
   - Table2 to tblOrders
   - Table3 to tblProducts
   - Table4 to tblCustomers
   - Table5 to tblCategories

e. **Click Next** to advance the wizard.

f. Observe that the primary keys have been generated by the wizard for each table.

5. **Make the necessary corrections and complete the wizard.**

a. **Click Next** to advance the wizard.

b. In the first row, from the Correction column drop-down list, **select the Cabin Tent row** to make the necessary corrections to the data.

c. From the Correction column drop-down list, **select (Leave As Is) for the other entries.**

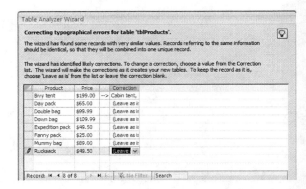

d. **Click Next** to advance the wizard.

e. In the Do You Want A Query section, **select the No Don't Create The Query option.**

f. **Click Finish** to complete the wizard.

g. **Close the Access Help window.**

6. **What is unusual about the design of foreign key fields in some tables?**

a) The foreign key fields contain more than one value.

b) The foreign key fields contain exactly one value.

c) The foreign key fields do not form part of the table relationships.

d) The foreign key fields are related to the primary keys of more than one table.

7. **Save and close the database.**

a. From the Office button menu, **choose Save As→Access 2007 Database.**

b. In the Microsoft Office Access message box, **click Yes** to close all open objects before converting the database to a different version.

c. **Save the database as *My structure***

d. **Close the database.**

TOPIC B
Create a Junction Table

Even after running the Table Analyzer Wizard, your data may be redundant and difficult to read. One way you can alleviate some of the redundancy in your tables is by using a junction table. In this topic, you will create a junction table.

Suppose you have two tables that already have a relationship, but that contain a great deal of redundant data. The redundant data can make the tables very difficult to understand, and they can substantially slow down database performance. The creation of a junction table can clean up your tables and allow your database to run much faster.

Many-to-Many Relationships

Definition:

A *many-to-many relationship* is a relationship between two tables where multiple records in one table can correspond to multiple records in the other table. The number of records that correspond can vary, but there must be at least two in each table.

Example:

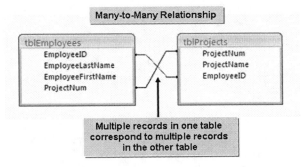

Junction Tables

Definition:

A *junction table* is a table that eliminates a many-to-many relationship between two other tables. The junction table's *primary key* will consist of both of the *foreign keys* from the other tables, thereby eliminating duplicate records. The number of fields included in the junction table may vary.

Example:

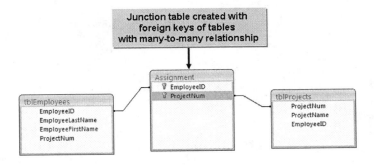

How to Create a Junction Table

Procedure Reference: Create a Junction Table

To create a junction table:

1. Create a new table with fields that are foreign key fields of the tables with the many-to-many relationship. The resultant table will be referred to as the junction table.

2. Designate the combination of those fields as the primary key of the junction table.

3. Save the table.

4. Create a query based on the original table having the many-to-many relationship. It should contain the fields present in the junction table.

5. Change the query type to an Append query.

6. In the Table Name drop-down list, select the Junction table.

7. Verify that the Append To row indicates the appropriate fields in the destination table.

8. Run the query and confirm the addition of the records.

9. If a message is displayed that states not all records can be appended, click Yes to ignore the errors and run the query.

10. If necessary, save and close the database.

ACTIVITY 1-2

Creating a Junction Table

Data Files:

JunctionTable.accdb

Before You Begin:

1. From the C:\084889Data\Structuring Existing Data folder, open the JunctionTable.accdb database.

2. If necessary, in the Access Options dialog box, in the Current Database category, change the Document Window Options to Tabbed Documents.

3. Exit Access and open the JunctionTable.accdb database again.

Scenario:

A member of the human resources staff has come to you for help. She was asked to keep track of the employees who are working on each internal project and create an Access database to do this. She realized that there was something wrong with the design of the tables because when table relationships were created, Access could not determine the relationship type. You will assist her by creating a junction table in the database.

What You Do	How You Do It
1. Create a junction table named **tblAssignments** with the fields **EmployeeID** and **ProjectNum** as the primary keys.	a. In the JunctionTable.accdb database, **create a table in Design view.**
	b. **Create a field, EmployeeID, with the text data type and field size of 4.**
	c. **Create a field, ProjectNum, with the text data type and field size of 4.**
	d. **Select the EmployeeID and ProjectNum fields.**
	e. On the Design contextual tab, in the Tools group, **click Primary Key** to make EmployeeID and ProjectNum the primary keys for the table.
	f. **Save the junction table with the name *tblAssignments***
	g. **Close the table's Design view.**

2. **Create a query that will add the EmployeeID and ProjectNum values from tblEmployees to the new table, tblAssignments.**

    a. **Create a new query in Design view.**

    b. **Add tblEmployees to the query from the Show Table dialog box and then close the Show Table dialog box.**

    c. **Add the EmployeeID and ProjectNum fields to the design grid.**

    d. In the Query Type group, **click Append.**

    e. In the Append dialog box, from the Table Name drop-down list, **select the tblAssignments table and click OK.**

    f. **Run the query.**

    g. In the Microsoft Office Access message box, **click Yes.**

    h. Observe that the Microsoft Office Access message box lists the reasons why Access cannot append all the records.

---

3. **True or False? Access was not able to append all the records to tblAssignments because the Append query contained duplicate records.**

    __ True

    __ False

---

4. **Continue the query and, when done, close it without saving changes to the design.**

    a. In the Microsoft Office Access message box, **click Yes.**

    b. **Close the query without saving the design.**

    c. **Open tblAssignments.**

    d. **Verify that there are 58 records.**

    e. **Close tblAssignments.**

TOPIC C
Improve Table Structure

You used the Table Analyzer Wizard and junction tables to rationalize table structure. However, over time, table structures may need to be changed, not just to rationalize them, but also to meet changing requirements of a company. In this topic, you will improve the table structure to meet a target design.

You have attempted to rationalize data across the table and this may require a change in the table structure. When you have to make changes to the existing table design and also append thousands of records from one table to another, attempting to make the changes without first fully understanding how to restructure them could lead to a lot of extra work.

How to Improve Table Structure

Procedure Reference: Improve Table Structure

To improve table structure:

1. Copy the structure of the existing tables to the new tables and name them appropriately.
2. Delete any unnecessary fields in the new tables and set the primary keys.
3. Create queries to move the required data to the new tables.
4. Delete the old tables from the database.
5. Rename the new tables.
6. Set the relationships between the new tables to enforce referential integrity.
7. If necessary, save and close the database.

ACTIVITY 1-3

Improving Table Structure by Modifying the Original Tables

Data Files:

ImproveTable.accdb

Setup:

From the C:\084889Data\Structuring Existing Data folder, open the ImproveTable.accdb database.

Scenario:

You have created the junction table tblAssignments and you need to change the original tables to comply with your design. There is a good chance that there will be some duplicate records and that the table relationships will need to be updated.

What You Do	How You Do It
1. Create a copy of the structure of the tables tblEmployees and tblProjects.	a. In the Navigation pane, **select tblEmployees** and, in the Clipboard group, **click the Copy button.**
	b. **Click Paste.**
	c. In the Paste Table As dialog box, in the Table Name text box, **type *TempEmployees***
	d. In the Paste Options section, **select Structure Only and click OK.**
	e. **Open TempEmployees** to confirm that you did not paste the data **and then close the table.**
	f. **Select tblProjects and copy it** to create the same structure with the name Temp-Projects.

2. **Delete the ProjectNum field and set EmployeeID as the primary key field of the TempEmployees table.**

   a. **Open TempEmployees in Design view.**

   b. **Delete the ProjectNum field.**

   c. In the Microsoft Office Access message box, **click Yes.**

   d. **Set the EmployeeID field as the primary key.**

   e. **Save and close the table design.**

3. **Delete the EmployeeID field and set ProjectNum as the primary key field of the TempProjects table.**

   a. **Open TempProjects in Design view.**

   b. **Delete the EmployeeID field.**

   c. **Set the ProjectNum field as the primary key.**

   d. **Save and close the table design.**

4. **Create and run a query that appends the data in the appropriate fields for the required tables.**

   a. **Create a new query in Design view.**

   b. **Add tblEmployees to the query.**

   c. **Close the Show Table dialog box.**

   d. **Add the EmployeeID, EmployeeLastName, and EmployeeFirstName fields to the design grid.**

   e. In the Query Type group, **click Append.**

   f. In the Append dialog box, from the Table Name drop-down list, **select TempEmployees and click OK.**

   g. **Run the query.**

   h. In the Microsoft Office Access message box, **click Yes** to append the rows to TempEmployees.

   i. In the Microsoft Office Access message box, **click Yes** to ignore the errors and run the query.

   j. **Close the Query Design window without saving the design.**

   k. **Open TempEmployees, verify that there are 47 unique records, and close the table.**

   l. **Create another query** to append the data in the ProjectNum and ProjectName fields from tblProjects to TempProjects. **Close the Query Design window without saving the design.**

   m. **Open TempProjects, verify that there are 10 records, and close the table.**

5. Rename TempEmployees to tblEmployees and TempProjects to tblProjects after deleting the tblEmployees and tblProjects tables.	a. In the Navigation pane, **select tblEmployees and press Delete.**
	b. In the Microsoft Office Access message box, **click Yes twice** to confirm the deletion and have Access delete its relationship to other tables.
	c. In the Navigation pane, **verify that tblProjects is selected and press Delete.**
	d. **Confirm the deletion.**
	e. **Rename the TempEmployees table** *tblEmployees*
	f. **Rename the TempProjects table** *tblProjects*
6. Set relationships between the tables, enforcing referential integrity. When creating one-to-many relationships, drag the fields from the one side to the many side.	a. On the Database Tools tab, in the Show/Hide group, **click Relationships.**
	b. In the Relationships group, **click Show Table, add tblAssignments, and close the Show Table dialog box.**
	c. **From tblEmployees, drag the EmployeeID field to the EmployeeID field in tblAssignments.**
	d. In the Edit Relationships dialog box, **check Enforce Referential Integrity and click Create.**
	e. **Create a relationship between the ProjectNum field in tblProjects and the ProjectNum field in tblAssignments, enforcing referential integrity.**
	f. **Close the Relationships window, saving the changes to the layout.**
	g. **Close the database.**

Lesson 1 Follow-up

In this lesson, you structured existing data. Effectively restructuring existing data will save you time with both troubleshooting a database and minimizing data redundancy.

1. **How would you use the Table Analyzer Wizard in your job?**

2. **How would you use normalization to improve the design of your database?**

2 Writing Advanced Queries

Lesson Time: 1 hour(s), 15 minutes

Lesson Objectives:

In this lesson, you will write advanced queries to analyze and summarize data.

You will:

- Create subqueries.
- Create unmatched and duplicate queries using the wizards.
- Group and summarize records using criteria.
- Summarize data using a crosstab query.
- Create a PivotTable and PivotChart to effectively summarize query data.

Introduction

You have used groups and totals in queries to summarize your data so that it has more meaning. You also used calculated fields to do aggregate calculations such as sums and averages. In this lesson, you will examine additional techniques that you can use to convert large amounts of data into meaningful information and to get the exact records you want when using a query to group and total data.

Because databases often contain thousands of records, the ability to summarize the data in effective ways is an important skill. The way you use different criteria will give you different results. Knowing other techniques for summarizing data will enable you to make the best presentation.

TOPIC A
Create Subqueries

You know how to structure data. Structuring data ensures data dependency and minimizes redundancy. After the data is logically stored, you may want to create advanced queries in order to retrieve subsets of data for viewing or analyzing. In this topic, you will learn to create subqueries, which is one way to simplify a complex query.

As a database manager, you may be asked to furnish information pertaining to a particular record, and the required information may be spread across tables. For example, if you are asked to retrieve the health plan for a particular employee, you may have to search through different tables to get the required information. You can simplify this task by using subqueries.

Subqueries

Definition:

A *subquery,* also known as an *inner query,* is a query that is contained within an outer query. A subquery is used when the value needed by the outer query's condition is unknown. The subquery retrieves the value and returns it to the outer query. Subqueries are always written within parentheses and can contain multiple inner queries, with each inner query enclosed within parentheses. You can sort and group records retrieved by the subquery.

Example:

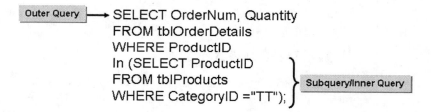

```
Outer Query ──→ SELECT OrderNum, Quantity
                FROM tblOrderDetails
                WHERE ProductID
                In (SELECT ProductID
                FROM tblProducts        ⎫ Subquery/Inner Query
                WHERE CategoryID ="TT");  ⎭
```

How to Create Subqueries

Procedure Reference: Create a Subquery in Design View

To create a subquery in Design view:

1. On the Create tab, in the Other group, click Query Design to create a query in Design view.

2. In the Show Table dialog box, select and add the table that will be used for the outer query.

3. Close the Show Table dialog box.

4. Add the required fields from the selected table.

5. Run the query and view the results of the outer query.

6. In the Criteria row of the matching field, type the SQL statement for the subquery.

7. Run the query.

8. Save the query.

SQL

Structured Query Language (SQL) is a computer language used to store, manipulate, and retrieve data stored in relational databases. SQL statements are not case sensitive. For example, SELECT is the same as select. The SELECT statement is used to select subsets of data from a table. There are also SQL statements to insert, delete, and modify data.

Procedure Reference: Create a Subquery in SQL View

To create a subquery in SQL view:

1. On the Create tab, in the Other group, click Query Design to create a query in Design view.

2. Close the Show Table dialog box.

3. On the Query Tools Design contextual tab, in the Results group, from the SQL View drop-down list, select SQL View.

4. In the SQL editor, type the SQL statement:

   ```
   SELECT <Field Name> FROM <Table1> WHERE <Field Name> In (SELECT <Field
   Name> FROM <Table 2> WHERE [condition]);
   ```

   The first SELECT statement is the outer query and the SELECT statement within the WHERE clause in parentheses is the subquery.

5. Run the query.

6. Observe the results.

7. Save the query.

ACTIVITY 2-1
Creating Subqueries

Data Files:

Summarize.accdb

Before You Begin:

From the C:\084889Data\Writing Advanced Queries folder, open the Summarize.accdb file.

Scenario:

The sales manager wants to know the number of orders for a particular category of product. You realize that tblOrderDetails has order numbers of all the categories. You do not want to spend time creating a join between the required tables. You would like the resultant query to display only the order numbers of a particular category.

What You Do	How You Do It
1. **Create a new query in Design view.**	a. On the Create tab, in the Other group, **click Query Design.**
	b. In the Show Table dialog box, on the Tables tab, **select tblOrderDetails and click Add.**
	c. **Close the Show Table dialog box.**
	d. From the tblOrderDetails table, **add the OrderNum and ProductID fields** to the outer query.
	e. **Run the outer query.**
	f. Observe the results: there are 730 records of all the categories.

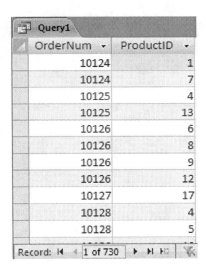

	g. **Switch to Design view.**
2. **Create a subquery using the Criteria row of the ProductID field to retrieve records pertaining to a particular category.**	a. In the query design grid, in the Criteria row of the ProductID field, **right-click and choose Zoom** to display the Zoom dialog box.
	b. In the Zoom dialog box, **type *In(SELECT ProductID FROM tblProducts WHERE CategoryID=TT)*** to include the subquery.
	c. **Click OK.**
3. **Test the query.**	a. **Run the query.**

b. Observe that there are 283 records show-
    ing the order numbers for all the products
    under the Category "TT."

OrderNum	ProductID
10124	1
10124	7
10127	17
10129	2
10129	17
10133	2
10133	7
10133	17
10136	2
10136	7
10137	1

Record: 1 of 283

c. **Save the query as** *qcustMySubquery*

d. **Close the query and the database.**

TOPIC B
Create Unmatched and Duplicate Queries

Previously, you created subqueries to retrieve records based on a condition. Sometimes, the condition may be to retrieve unrelated or duplicate records in a table or query. These tasks can easily be done with the help of Microsoft® Office Access™ 2007 wizards. In this topic, you will create queries in order to search for unmatched and duplicate records in a table or query.

As the administrator of a database, one of your jobs will be to keep the database working as efficiently as possible. A major cause of database slowdown is erroneous or duplicate data in a table. You can keep these problems to a minimum by running advanced queries in order to search out the errant data.

The Find Unmatched Query Wizard

When two tables or queries are compared, the *Find Unmatched Query Wizard* finds records in one table or query that have no related records in another table or query. The wizard gives you the option to select the field to be compared. The resultant query displays only those values that are unique to the first table, based on the field being compared.

The Find Duplicates Query Wizard

The *Find Duplicates Query Wizard* creates a query that finds records with duplicate field values in a single table or query. For example, in the Candidate table, if you want to retrieve a list of candidates who have applied from a particular city, say Mexico City, then the wizard retrieves the candidates from Mexico City. When only one field, City, is selected, the resultant query displays the number of duplicates under the default field name, NumberOfDups.

How to Create Unmatched and Duplicate Queries

Procedure Reference: Create an Unmatched Query

To create an unmatched query:

1. Open the database.
2. On the Create tab, in the Other group, click Query Wizard to display the New Query dialog box.
3. In the New Query dialog box, select Find Unmatched Query Wizard and click OK to open the Find Unmatched Query Wizard.
4. In the Tables list box, select the table or query you want to compare. Click Next.
5. In the Tables list box, select the table or query that contains related records.
6. In the Fields In <Name> list box on the left, select the field, and in the Fields In <Name> list box on the right, select the matching field.
7. Click the <=> button to establish a comparison between the fields selected and click Next.
8. In the Available Fields list box, double-click the fields you want in the query results. Click Next.
9. In the What Would You Like To Name Your Query text box, type the name of the query and click Finish to close the wizard.

Microsoft® Office Access™ 2007: Level 3 (Second Edition)

10. Observe that the resultant query contains values that are not common to both tables.

Procedure Reference: Create a Duplicate Query

To create a duplicate query:

1. Open the database.
2. On the Create tab, in the Other group, click Query Wizard to display the New Query dialog box.
3. In the New Query dialog box, select Find Duplicates Query Wizard and click OK to open the Find Duplicates Query Wizard.
4. In the Tables list box, select the table or query that contains duplicate field values. Click Next.
5. In the Available Fields list box, double-click the fields to add them to the Duplicate-Value Fields list box. Click Next.
6. In the Available Fields list box, double-click the fields to move them to the Additional Query Fields list box to have additional fields in the resultant query.
7. In the What Do You Want To Name Your Query text box, type the name of the query and click Finish to close the wizard.
8. Observe the default field created.

ACTIVITY 2-2

Creating Queries to Search for Unmatched and Duplicate Records

Data Files:

Contacts.accdb

Before You Begin:

From the C:\084889Data\Writing Advanced Queries folder, open the Contacts.accdb file.

Scenario:

Up to this point, each member of the sales team has kept a separate contact list in Access for all his or her clients. Moving forward, the management would like to compile one complete list for all sales contacts. Since the sales force is not extremely well-versed in Access, you know there might be a few problems you will run into before combining the lists. Before you combine the tables, you want to make sure there are no duplicate records of company names in all tables, and you also want to check the individual tables for duplicates.

What You Do	How You Do It
1. **Open the Find Unmatched Query Wizard.**	a. On the Create tab, in the Other group, **click Query Wizard** to open the New Query dialog box.
	b. In the New Query dialog box, **select Find Unmatched Query Wizard and click OK.**
2. **Compare Susan's Contacts table and John's Contacts table.**	a. In the Tables list box, **select Table: Susan's Contacts and click Next.**
	b. On the second page, in the Tables list box, **verify that Table: John's Contacts is selected and click Next.**
3. **Select the CompanyName field for making the comparison.**	a. In the Fields In 'Susan Contacts' list box on the left, **select the CompanyName field.**
	b. In the Fields In 'John's Contacts': list box on the right, **select the CompanyName field.**
	c. **Click the <=> button** to match the fields.
	d. **Click Next.**

4. **Select only the matched field to appear in the resultant query.**

   a. In the Available Fields list box, **double-click the CompanyName field.**

   b. **Click Next.**

   c. Observe the default name for the query and **click Finish** to complete the wizard.

   d. Observe that the query displays nine company names that appear in Susan's contacts but not in John's.

   e. **Close the query.**

5. **Open the Find Duplicates Query Wizard.**

   a. On the Create tab, in the Other group, **click Query Wizard.**

   b. In the New Query dialog box, **select Find Duplicates Query Wizard and click OK.**

6. **Find the duplicates in the CompanyName field.**

   a. In the Tables list box, **select Table: Susan's Contacts and click Next.**

   b. In the Available Fields list box, **double-click CompanyName** to move the field to the Duplicate-Value Fields list box and **click Next.**

   c. Because you do not want any field other than CompanyName to be displayed, **click Next.**

   d. Observe the default name for the query and **click Finish** to complete the wizard.

e. Observe that the query shows the three duplicate records in Susan's contacts and how many times they are repeated.

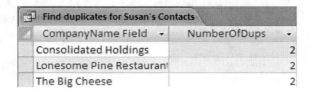

CompanyName Field	NumberOfDups
Consolidated Holdings	2
Lonesome Pine Restaurant	2
The Big Cheese	2

f. **Close the query and the database.**

TOPIC C
Group and Summarize Records Using Criteria

You have used the Find Unmatched Query Wizard and Find Duplicates Query Wizard to search for duplicate and unmatched records. There may be times when searches have to be made and customizing the search may be a better option. In this topic, you will see how you can search for a particular group of records using the Criteria row in different ways.

Imagine that you are working with a 100,000-record database, but you need to find only a very small subset of those records that match a specific ID number. Using the Criteria row can take what would be a very tedious task and make it happen in just a few seconds.

The Criteria Row

The Criteria row appears in the design grid when a query is viewed in Design view. This row allows you to apply conditions to your queries. You can limit the records returned by a query to only those that meet specific requirements that you declare in the Criteria row. Some criteria are simple and use basic operators and constants. Other criteria are complex and use functions, special operators, and field references.

How to Group and Summarize Records Using Criteria

Procedure Reference: Summarize Data Using the Criteria Row

To summarize data using the Criteria row:

1. Open the query in Design view.
2. From the tables displayed, select the fields to be included in the query.
3. In the Criteria row of the required field, enter the condition.
4. Run the query and examine the results.
5. Change the condition in the Criteria row and run the query again to view different results.
6. Save and close the query.

ACTIVITY 2-3
Summarizing Records in Different Ways with Criteria

Data Files:

Criteria.accdb

Before You Begin:

From the C:\084889Data\Writing Advanced Queries folder, open the Criteria.accdb file.

Scenario:

You have been asked to provide some data about the purchasing volume of your customers. You want to see how many of your products each customer has bought so that you can then focus on the largest volumes. You have been asked to:

- Look at the total amount of each product purchased by each customer.

- Create a list of customers and products where the total purchases were greater than $5,000.

- From the list of customers and products greater than $5,000, list only the records dated March 1, 2001 or later.

What You Do	How You Do It
1. Open the query qtotCustomerTotals and switch to Design view.	**a. Double-click qtotCustomerTotals.**
	b. Observe that there are 70 records. Records are grouped first on Customer Name and then on Product.

CustomerName	Product	TotalSales
All Weather Sports	Cabin tent	$63,957.54
All Weather Sports	Dome tent	$3,870.00
All Weather Sports	Down bag	$3,924.00
All Weather Sports	Mummy bag	$3,240.00
All Weather Sports	Screen house	$43,884.00
Camping Unlimited	Bivy tent	$17,114.00
Camping Unlimited	Cabin tent	$7,799.70
Camping Unlimited	Camp bag	$7,438.76
Camping Unlimited	Day pack	$5,590.00
Camping Unlimited	Dome tent	$25,542.00
Camping Unlimited	Double bag	$12,098.79

Record: 1 of 70   No Filter   Search

	c. **Switch to Design view.**
	d. If necessary, **increase the TotalSales column width so that you can view the sales values clearly.**
	e. Observe the total amount of each product purchased by the customers.

2. What is the purpose of the calculated expression?

a) The expression creates a calculated field named Total Sales.

b) The expression formats the result with the dollar sign ($).

c) The expression totals the result for each group of products.

d) The expression takes Quantity and Price from just one table.

3. Find the products with sales greater than $5,000.	a. In the Criteria row of the Total Sales field, **type >5000**
	b. **Run the query.**

c. Observe that there are 35 records with sales greater than $5,000.

CustomerName	Product	TotalSales
All Weather Sports	Cabin tent	$63,957.54
All Weather Sports	Screen house	$43,884.00
Camping Unlimited	Bivy tent	$17,114.00
Camping Unlimited	Cabin tent	$7,799.70
Camping Unlimited	Camp bag	$7,438.76
Camping Unlimited	Day pack	$5,590.00
Camping Unlimited	Dome tent	$25,542.00
Camping Unlimited	Double bag	$12,098.79
Camping Unlimited	Down bag	$18,094.00
Good Gear	Bivy tent	$7,960.00
Good Gear	Camp bag	$6,958.84

Record: 1 of 35   No Filter   Search

d. **Switch to Design view.**

---

4. **List the records dated 3/1/01 or later.**

a. In tblOrders, **double-click the Date field.**

b. **Click in the Total row of the Date field,** and from the drop-down list, **select Where.**

c. In the Criteria row of the Date field, **click and type *>3/1/01***

d. **Run the query.**

e. Observe that 15 matching records are displayed.

f. **Save and close the query and then close the database.**

TOPIC D

Summarize Data Using a Crosstab Query

You know how valuable a totals query can be in summarizing data. Another type of query, a crosstab query, enables you to summarize values and display them in a compact, spreadsheet-like format. In this topic, you will summarize data using a crosstab query.

Because different areas of a business use a database, they will all have specific needs for how their data is displayed. For instance, the sales department of your company might need to determine their biggest customer. They would appreciate it if you could provide this data with customer names as row headings, the products as column headings, and the total quantity purchased against the intersection of each customer and product. With the help of a crosstab query, you can accomplish this task easily.

The Crosstab Query

Definition:

A *crosstab query* is a query that calculates and summarizes table data in a spreadsheet-like format. Unlike a select query, where values are listed below the field name, a crosstab query displays values of a field as a row heading, a column heading, or at the intersection of the row and column. Using the Crosstab Query Wizard, the user can choose what data will be displayed for the row and column headings and how the intersecting data is calculated. You can use a crosstab query to calculate the sum, average, count of records, count of values, maximum value, standard deviation, and variance of data.

Example:

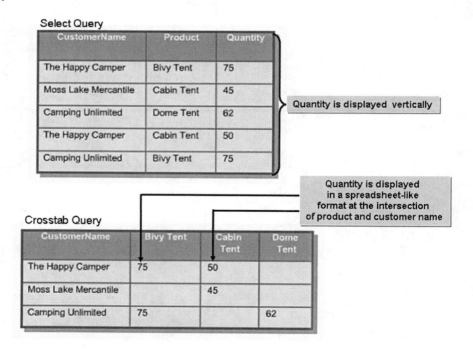

How to Summarize Data Using a Crosstab Query

Procedure Reference: Summarize Data with a Crosstab Query

To summarize data with a crosstab query:

1. On the Create tab, in the Other group, click Query Wizard to display the New Query dialog box.

2. In the New Query dialog box, select Crosstab Query Wizard and click OK to open the Crosstab Query Wizard.

3. On the Crosstab Query Wizard page, select the query and click Next.

4. In the Available Fields list box, select the field(s) with the values you want as row headings. You can select up to three fields. Click Next.

5. Select the field with the values you want as column headings. Click Next.

 You need to select the interval if you select the Date field as the column heading.

6. In the Fields list box, select the field containing the data you want summarized according to the values in the rows and columns. In the Functions list box, select the summary operation to be performed. Click Next.

7. Enter the query name in the What Do You Want To Name Your Query text box and click Finish, which will run the query.

8. Close the query.

ACTIVITY 2-4
Summarizing Data with a Crosstab Query

Data Files:

Crosstab.accdb

Before You Begin:

From the C:\084889Data\Writing Advanced Queries folder, open the Crosstab.accdb file.

Scenario:

The sales manager wants to know how well each product in a category has sold in each month of the first quarter. You have created a select query to extract the records you need, and now you need to figure out how to summarize them to answer the sales manager's question.

What You Do	How You Do It
1. Familiarize yourself with the design of the query qselQ1Sales.	a. **Open the qselQ1Sales query in Design view.**
	b. Observe that the query selects from several tables, the Category, Product, and Date fields with the criterion that the sales date is in the first quarter, and also that it calculates the amount of each sale.
	c. **Run the query.**
	d. Observe that 730 records are displayed.
	e. **Save and close the query.**
2. Start the Crosstab Query Wizard and base the new query on qselQ1Sales.	a. On the Create tab, in the Other group, **click Query Wizard.**
	b. In the New Query dialog box, **select the Crosstab Query Wizard and click OK.**
	c. In the View section, **select Queries** to display the list of queries.
	d. From the list of queries, **select Query: qselQ1Sales and click Next.**

3.	Select Category and Product as row headings.	a.	In the Available Fields list box, **verify that the Category field is selected and click the > button.**
		b.	**Verify that the Product field is selected and click the > button.**
		c.	**Click Next.**
4.	Select Date and Month as the column headings.	a.	In the Available Fields list box, **verify that Date is selected and click Next.**
		b.	**Select Month and click Next.**
5.	Select Sum as the function.	a.	In the Fields list box, **verify that Sale is selected,** and in the Functions list box, **select Sum.**
		b.	**Click Next and then click Finish** to save the query using the default name.
		c.	**Switch to Design view.**
6.	Change the query property to delete extra columns.	a.	**Click in the space above the design grid,** and from the Show/Hide group, **display the Property Sheet pane.**
		b.	In the Column Headings row, **right-click and choose Zoom** to display the Zoom dialog box.
		c.	In the Zoom dialog box, **delete all the months after the closing double quotes of Mar and click OK.**
		d.	**Close the Property Sheet pane and run the query.**

7. **What features do you notice in the design created by the wizard?**

   a) The Crosstab Query Wizard created a totals query that also has a crosstab row.

   b) Each field is designated as Row Heading, Column Heading, or Value.

   c) The Date values are formatted as the three-letter abbreviation for the month and are grouped on that value.

   d) The Crosstab Query Wizard does not sort the resultant data.

8. Move the Total Of Sale column so that it is the last column.

   a. Select the Total Of Sale column and move it to the right of the Mar column.

   b. Save and close the query.

   c. Close the database.

TOPIC E
Create a PivotTable and a PivotChart

You saw how a crosstab query can be a powerful tool for summarizing data. In this topic, you will examine how to create objects that summarize data in much the same way as a crosstab query, but in a format the Access user can interact with to see data in different ways.

As a database manager, you may have to analyze large amounts of data. You might have to compare data and it could sometimes be nearly impossible to manually compare values. Interactive PivotTables and PivotCharts enable you to manipulate summary data and therefore can save you from having to create multiple queries and reports to achieve the same results.

The PivotTable

Definition:

A *PivotTable* is a database view in Access that allows you to summarize and examine data in a datasheet or form. It is used to group values as rows and columns with a calculated value at the intersection of each row and column. A PivotTable is created by dragging fields to the appropriate area on the design screen. Data can also be broken down to different levels of detail, such as showing earnings by year, quarter, or month.

Example:

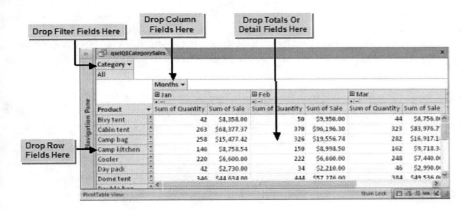

The PivotChart

Definition:

A *PivotChart* is a database view in Access that displays a graphical analysis of data in a datasheet, PivotTable, or form. It displays a summary of data in different chart formats and enables interactive analysis of data. A PivotChart is created by dragging fields to the appropriate area on the design screen. Data can be broken down to different levels of detail, and unwanted items can be hidden from view.

Example:

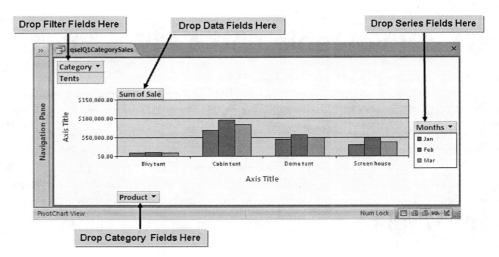

PivotTable View

You can access PivotTable view from the Views group on the Home tab. A PivotTable has four areas for dropping fields whose values will be summarized.

Drop Area	Description
Drop Filter Fields Here	In this drop area, you can drag and drop fields from a table or query, and the values of the fields selected will be used as a filter for your Pivot-Table.
Drop Column Fields Here	In this drop area, you can drag and drop fields from a table or query, and the values of the fields selected will be displayed as column headings.
Drop Row Fields Here	In this drop area, you can drag and drop fields from a table or query, and the values of the fields selected will be displayed as row headings.
Drop Totals Or Detail Fields Here	In this drop area, you can drag and drop fields with values that will be displayed in a calculated or summarized format. These values will be displayed at the intersection of a row and column.

PivotChart View

You can access PivotChart view from the Views group on the Home tab. PivotChart view has four areas for dropping fields whose values will be summarized in a chart format. A table, query, or PivotTable can be viewed as a PivotChart.

Drop Area	Description
Drop Filter Fields Here	In this drop area, you can drag and drop fields from a table or query, and the values of the fields selected will be used as a filter for your PivotChart.
Drop Data Fields Here	In the drop area, drag and drop fields with values that you want to show along the Y-axis. For example, in a bar chart, the height of the bars depends on these values.
Drop Category Fields Here	In this drop area, drag and drop fields with values that you want to show along the X-axis. For example, in a bar chart, the width of the bars depends on these values.
Drop Series Fields Here	In this drop area, drag and drop fields with values that will form the legend of the graph. For example, if you have selected the Date By Month field as columns in the PivotTable, then the legend displayed will be Jan, Feb, Mar, and so on.

How to Create a PivotTable and a PivotChart

Procedure Reference: Create a PivotTable

To create a PivotTable:

1. Open the query.
2. On the Home tab, in the Views group, from the View drop-down list, select PivotTable View.
3. From the PivotTable Field List pane, drag and drop fields to the following drop areas:
   - Drop Filter Fields Here
   - Drop Column Fields Here
   - Drop Row Fields Here
4. In the Drop Totals Or Detail Fields Here drop area, select the field(s) with the values you want to calculate.
5. On the PivotTable Tools Design contextual tab, in the Tools group, from the Formulas drop-down list, select Create Calculated Total or Create Calculated Detail Field.
6. In the Properties dialog box, on the Calculation tab, in the Name text area, type the required calculation and click Change.
7. In the Properties dialog box, on the Format tab, from the Number drop-down list, specify a format. Close the Properties dialog box.
8. On the PivotTable Tools Design contextual tab, in the Tools group, from the AutoCalc drop-down list, select a function.

9. On the PivotTable Tools Design contextual tab, in the Show/Hide group, you can select Hide Details.

10. Click the expand indicators (+) of the required fields to further break up the data. For example, you can expand the Date field to show quarterly values.

11. Use the filter fields to view selected data.

12. If necessary, modify the view to suit your information needs.

    ● Expand the view of the fields using the expand indicator next to the field.

    ● In the column heading area, click the required fields and drag them out of the window to remove unnecessary fields.

13. Save the PivotTable.

Procedure Reference: Create a PivotChart

To create a PivotChart based on a PivotTable:

1. View the PivotTable.

2. On the Home tab, in the Views group, from the View drop-down list, select PivotChart View.

3. Select only one value from the Filter field's drop-down list.

4. If desired, interchange the row and column fields and observe the change.

5. On the PivotChart Tools Design contextual tab, in the Type group, select Change Chart Type to view different charts.

6. In the Properties dialog box, on the Format tab, in the Caption text box, change the axis titles as desired.

7. Close the Properties dialog box and then close the database.

ACTIVITY 2-5
Creating a PivotTable

Data Files:

PivotTable.accdb

Before You Begin:

From the C:\084889Data\Writing Advanced Queries folder, open the PivotTable.accdb file.

Scenario:

You have submitted the summary of the sales data to your vice president of sales for review. She has asked that you use Access tools and provide the data in a table format that she can manipulate and view differently.

She has also mentioned that the table view should have the following parameters:

- The Category field should be a filter.
- The Product field should be the rows.
- The Date By Month field should be the columns.
- The Detail Data area should display the total sales.
- The total sales for the tents category should be displayed in Table view.

What You Do	How You Do It
1. **Open the qselQ1CategorySales query and create a PivotTable view with the required parameters.**	a. **Open the qselQ1CategorySales query.**
	b. On the Home tab, in the Views group, from the View drop-down list, **select PivotTable View** to open the PivotTable Tools Design window.
	c. In the PivotTable Field List pane, **select the Category field and drag it to the Drop Filter Fields Here area.**
	d. In the PivotTable Field List pane, **select the Product field and drag it to the Drop Row Fields Here area.**
	e. **Select the Date By Month field and drag it to the Drop Column Fields Here area** to display Years with the drill buttons and Grand Total.

f. **Drag the Price and Quantity fields to the Drop Totals Or Detail Fields Here area** to display Price and Sum Of Quantity.

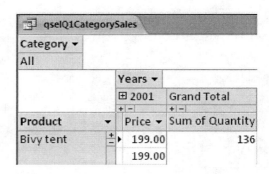

g. **Close the PivotTable Field List pane.**

2. **Create a calculated detail field for the Price and Quantity fields.**

a. On the PivotTable Tools Design contextual tab, in the Tools group, from the Formulas drop-down list, **select Create Calculated Detail Field** to display the Calculated column as well as the Properties dialog box.

b. Observe that a field named Calculated is automatically created adjacent to the Price field.

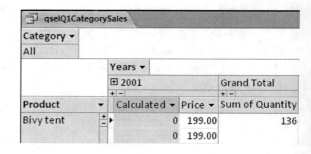

c. In the Properties dialog box, on the Calculation tab, in the Name text area, **select 0, type *Price*Quantity* and click Change.**

d. Observe the change in the Calculated column.

3.	Change the caption of the Calculated field to Sale and prefix the dollar sign ($) to the sales figures.	a.	In the Properties dialog box, on the Captions tab, in the Caption text box, **select Calculated, type** *Sale* **and press Enter** to change the caption to Sale.
		b.	On the Format tab, from the Number drop-down list, **select Currency** to prefix the dollar sign ($) to the sales figures.
		c.	**Close the Properties dialog box.**
4.	Designate the Sale field as a Sum calculation and then hide details in PivotTable view.	a.	**Verify that the Sale column is selected.**
		b.	On the PivotTable Tools Design contextual tab, in the Tools group, **click AutoCalc and select Sum** to display the Sum Of Sale column.
		c.	On the PivotTable Tools Design contextual tab, in the Show/Hide group, **click Hide Details.**
5.	Expand the view of 2001 and Qtr1 and remove the Years and Quarters column heading labels from PivotTable view.	a.	**Expand the view of 2001** to display the first quarter.
		b.	**Expand Qtr1** to view the Jan, Feb, and Mar columns.
		c.	In the column heading area, **click Years and drag it anywhere outside the table area, until an X appears.**
		d.	In the column heading area, **click Quarters and drag it out of the window until an X appears** to remove the Qtr1 field.
6.	View Quantity and Sale for the category Tents.	a.	**Click the Category drop-down arrow and uncheck (All).**
		b.	**Check Tents and click OK.**
		c.	Observe that only the products in the category Tents are displayed.
		d.	**Click the Category drop-down arrow, check (All), and click OK** to display all the categories.
		e.	**Save and close the qselQ1CategorySales query.**
		f.	**Close the database.**

ACTIVITY 2-6

Working with a PivotChart

Data Files:

PivotChart.accdb

Before You Begin:

From the C:\084889Data\Writing Advanced Queries folder, open the PivotChart.accdb file.

Scenario:

You would like to give the vice president of sales as many options as possible for viewing the summary of data for the Tents category. You know she has asked for graphical representations of data in the past.

What You Do	How You Do It
1. **Open qselQ1CategorySales and verify the presence of the Pivot-Table.**	a. **Double-click qselQ1CategorySales.** b. On the Home tab, in the Views group, from the View drop-down list, **select PivotTable View.** c. Observe the data displayed in the Pivot-Table format.
2. **Create a PivotChart view of the data.**	a. In the Views group, from the View drop-down list, **select PivotChart View** to convert the PivotTable data into a PivotChart. b. If necessary, **close the Chart Field List pane.** c. On the PivotChart Tools Design contextual tab, in the Show/Hide group, **click Legend** to display the legend as Jan, Feb, and Mar with different colors.

3. **View the chart for the Tents category with Months in the horizontal axis and Products in the vertical bars.**

   a. **Click the Category drop-down arrow and uncheck (All).**

   b. **Check Tents and click OK.**

   c. **Select Months and drag it next to Product on the X-axis.**

   d. **Click Product and drag it to the Drop Series Fields Here area** to display the legend.

   e. **View the PivotChart in PivotTable view** to see the changes reflected in the Pivot-Table.

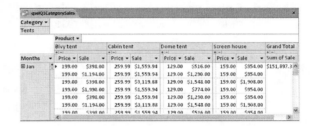

4. **Pivot the chart again so Months are the Series fields and Products are the Category fields.**

   a. In the Views group, from the View drop-down list, **select PivotChart View.**

   b. **Click Months and drag it below the Product field.**

   c. **Click Product and drag it to the Drop Category Fields Here area.**

   d. **Drag Sum Of Quantity and drop it below the qselQICategorySales tab.**

5. **View the data as different types of column charts and finish with a 3-D column chart.**

   a. **Right-click in the Chartspace area and choose Change Chart Type.**

   b. In the Properties dialog box, on the Type tab, **select Bar Chart** and, from the right pane, **select the second bar chart in the first row.**

   c. **Similarly try selecting different chart types and observe the output.**

d. Finally, in the right pane of the Column chart, **select the first column chart in the second row** to view the output in a 3-D column chart.

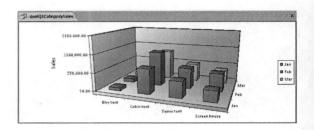

6. **Add Sales as the vertical axis title and delete the horizontal axis title.**

a. In the Chart window, **click the vertical axis title.**

b. In the Properties dialog box, on the Format tab, in the Caption text box, **select Axis Title, type *Sales* and press Enter.**

c. **Select the horizontal axis title and press Delete.**

d. **Close the Properties dialog box.**

e. **Save and close qselQ1CategorySales.**

f. **Close the database.**

Lesson 2 Follow-up

In this lesson, you created advanced queries. Queries will help you to summarize your data in many different ways. Using every available summary technique, you can make the most effective presentation for your audience.

1. **What are the ways in which you can use unmatched and duplicate queries?**

2. **Will PivotCharts and PivotTables be useful on the job? Why?**

3 Simplifying Tasks with Macros

Lesson Time: 1 hour(s), 10 minutes

Lesson Objectives:

In this lesson, you will create and revise Microsoft® Office Access™ 2007 macros.

You will:

● Create a macro that opens a form from an existing form to display records.

● Attach a macro to a form.

● Restrict records by adding a condition.

● Create a macro that makes data entry mandatory to ensure data validation.

● Create a macro that inputs data automatically when a predefined condition is fulfilled.

Introduction

Having explored different ways to structure and write advanced queries, you are now going to turn your attention toward database usability. You are going to make it easier for database users to access and interact with the data stored in your database. In this lesson, you will learn to create macros that simplify database activities, automate tasks using a macro, and use macros to add interactivity to your database applications.

When working on a database, you may need to perform repetitive tasks such as inserting data into forms or tables, creating tables, opening forms, or generating reports. By creating and using macros, you can automate these tasks and save yourself valuable time and effort.

TOPIC A
Create a Macro

You may need to perform many repetitive actions while building a database. These repetitive tasks can often consume the bulk of the time you spend using Access. You can automate these tasks and save time by creating macros.

Creating a macro is like programming your car radio. Before you program in your favorite radio stations, you are stuck searching for the next good song by endlessly turning the tuning dial or scanning through each and every station. Because this can be so tedious, it is wise to take a few minutes to program in all of your favorite stations, so that finding your preferred music and news is as easy as pressing a button. It is the same with creating macros. If you take the time to create them, you will soon be moving around quickly, thereby saving time and enjoying the power that macros add to your work in Access.

Macros

Definition:

A *macro* is a tool that performs a series of actions that automate a process or a set of tasks. Macros can be created in several of the applications in the Microsoft Office suite. In Access, macros can be created for tasks such as opening a form for entering customer records, running a query and printing the results, finding and filtering records for a report, or validating data. All macros are programmed to run on the occurrence of an event on a control, and they are therefore linked to the event and the control.

Example:

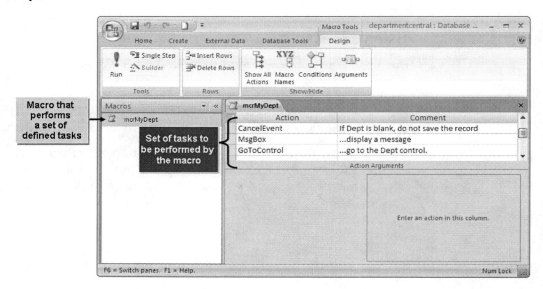

The Macro Builder Window

The Macro Builder window is used to create and modify macros. The upper part of the window is where you can add the actions, comments, and conditions in the respective columns. In the Action column, you can specify the action commands that you want the macro to perform, such as opening a form. In the Comment column, you can describe each action that has been added to the macro. Comments are optional, but they make it easier to understand and maintain the macro. In the Condition column, you can enter the expressions that control when an action is performed. The lower part of the window, called the Action Arguments pane, is where you can specify arguments for an action.

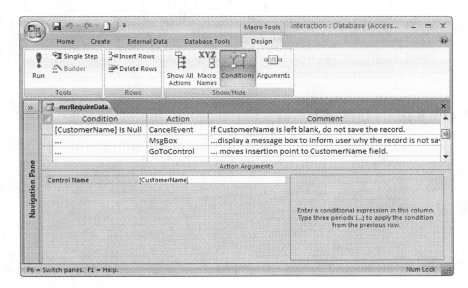

Figure 3-1: *The Macro Builder window.*

Macro Actions

Definition:

A *macro action* is a self-contained instruction that can automate tasks and forms the basic unit of a macro. Macro actions, which resemble menu commands, are selected manually after creating a macro. You can create a macro with one or more actions to perform a specific task or a series of tasks. Macro actions may require additional information called action arguments, which determine how the macro performs the task.

Example:

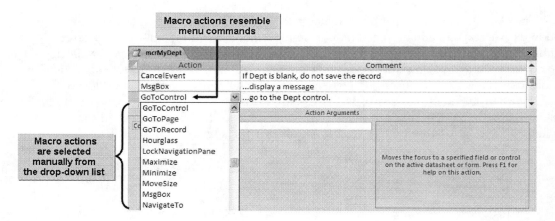

Types of Macro Actions

Access has 71 macro actions, which can be selected from the drop-down list in the Action column of the Macro Builder window. There are a few commonly used macro actions.

Action	Purpose
AddMenu	Adds a drop-down menu to a menu bar. Used in forms and reports.
Echo	Controls whether a macro updates the screen.
CancelEvent	Cancels the event that runs the current macro.
FindRecord	Finds a record that meets your criteria.
GoToControl	Changes focus to a particular control.
GoToRecord	Jumps to a specified record.
MoveSize	Moves or resizes a window.
MsgBox	Displays a message box.
OpenForm	Opens a form.
SetValue	Specifies the contents of a field, control, or property.

Action Arguments

Arguments provide additional information to macro actions on how to carry out an action. They are basically settings of a macro action that control the operations of a macro. The arguments that are listed depend on the action you have chosen. Each action has different arguments, but only some actions require arguments. Action arguments can be viewed in the Arguments column in the upper part of the Macro Builder window but cannot be edited there.

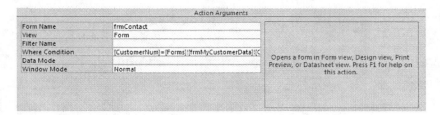

Figure 3-2: The Action Arguments pane.

How to Create a Macro

Procedure Reference: Create a Macro

To create a macro:

1. Open the Macro Builder window.

    ● On the Create tab, in the Other group, click Macro.

    ● Or, click the Build button of any event property to display the Choose Builder window. Select Macro Builder and click OK.

2. On the Design contextual tab, in the Show/Hide group, click Show All Actions.

3. From the drop-down list in the Actions column, select the macro actions you want the macro to perform.

4. For each action, define the action arguments.

5. Save the macro.

6. Test the macro by double-clicking it in the Navigation pane and verifying its functionality.

ACTIVITY 3-1
Creating a Macro to Display a Form

Data Files:

Macro.accdb

Before You Begin:

From the C:\084889Data\Macros folder, open the Macro.accdb file.

Scenario:

The manager of the sales department has come to you for help with the department's Access database in order to help sales agents save time and work efficiently. Currently most customer data is accessed through one form, but the customer contact name is accessed through another. Sales agents must search through the Contact form to find the name of their contact at each customer's company. Sales agents could save time and be more efficient in setting up their calls if they could access the customer Contact form from the corresponding CustomerData form.

What You Do	How You Do It
1. **Hide the results until the macro is completed.**	a. On the Create tab, in the Other group, **click Macro** to launch a new Macro Builder window.
	b. On the Design contextual tab, in the Show/Hide group, **click Show All Actions.**
	c. In the first row of the Action column, **click the drop-down arrow and select Echo.**

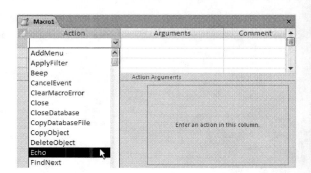

d. At the bottom of the Macro Builder window, in the Action Arguments pane, **click in the Echo On text box,** and from the drop-down list, **select No** to hide the results of the macro until it is finished.

2. **Add the OpenForm action.**

    a. In the second row of the Action column, **click** to display the drop-down list **and select OpenForm.**

    b. In the Action Arguments pane, **click the Form Name property box.**

    c. From the Form Name drop-down list, **select frmContact** so that the form name is displayed in the Form Name text box.

3. **Save the macro as mcrMyContact.**

    a. **Click the Save button.**

    b. **Name the macro *mcrMyContact* and click OK.**

    c. **Close the Macro Builder window.**

    d. In the Navigation pane, **click the Forms drop-down arrow and select Macros.**

    e. In the Navigation pane, **double-click the macro mcrMyContact** to execute it.

    f. Observe that the macro opens frmContact.

    g. **Close the form window.**

TOPIC B
Attach a Macro

You have now created a macro to automate a task. Although the macro is saved in the database, it has not yet been put to use in your database. You can now put your macro to work by attaching it to a command button in a form. In this topic, you will attach a macro to a command button in a form.

Creating and saving the macro in the database is a large part of your work. However, a macro on its own serves no purpose. By attaching the macros you create to the appropriate command buttons, you can give users a means of launching and running them and thereby completing tasks that were intended to be automated by the macro.

Object Events

Definition:

An *object event* is an action that is triggered by a user on a database object. Object events are used to trigger macros, which then perform the tasks they were designed to perform. Attaching an event to a macro will ensure that the macro runs when the particular event occurs on the database object.

Example:

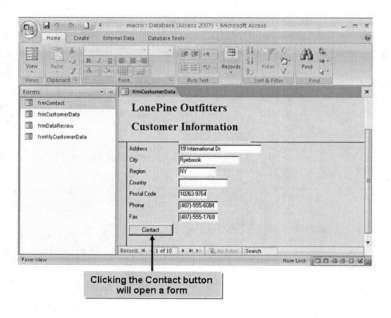

Clicking the Contact button will open a form

Object Event Categories

Forms, reports, and controls are the only objects in which Access recognizes events. These events can be categorized into several groups.

Event Group	Examples
Window events	Opening, closing, or resizing a window are examples of window events.

Event Group	Examples
Data events	Updating or deleting forms, records, or any data are examples of data events.
Focus events	Activating, entering, or exiting are examples of focus events.
Keyboard events	Pressing or releasing a key are examples of keyboard events.
Mouse events	Clicking or double-clicking the mouse buttons are examples of mouse events.
Print events	Format and print are examples of print events.
Error and timing events	Occurrence of an error or lapse of some time between events are examples of error and timing events.

How to Attach a Macro

Procedure Reference: Attach a Macro to a Command Button

To attach a macro to a command button:

1. Open the form in Design view.
2. After deactivating the Use Control Wizard button, add a command button.
3. If necessary, change the caption of the command button.
4. Decide when the macro should execute and to which event it should be attached.
5. Display the Property Sheet pane for the command button.
6. In the Property Sheet pane, select the Event tab.
7. Click in the On Click text box.
8. From the On Click text box's drop-down list, select the macro you want to run when the object event occurs.
9. Close the Property Sheet pane.
10. Save the form.
11. Test the object event.

ACTIVITY 3-2
Attaching a Macro to a Command Button

Data Files:

Macro.accdb

Before You Begin:

If necessary, from the C:\084889Data\Macros folder, open the Macro.accdb file.

Scenario:

You have created the mcrMyContact macro that opens the frmContact form, just as the sales manager had asked. But you see that there is no way of launching the frmContact form from the frmCustomer Data form, despite creating a macro to automate the task. Therefore, you decide to attach the macro to the form.

What You Do	How You Do It
1. Add a command button to the form frmCustomer Data.	a. **Open the frmCustomerData form in Design view.**
	b. On the Design contextual tab, in the Controls group, **click the Use Control Wizards button** to deselect it and thereby prevent the Command Button Wizard from launching.
	c. On the Design contextual tab, in the Controls group, **click Button.**
	d. In the Design View window, below the Fax field, **click the form** to create a command button.
	e. On the Design contextual tab, in the Tools group, **click Property Sheet** to display the Property Sheet pane for the command button.
	f. On the All tab, in the Name text box, **select the existing text and type** *cmdContact*
	g. In the Caption text box, **select the existing text and type** *Contact*

2. **When should the mcrMyContact macro be executed?**
   a) When the form is closed.
   b) When the button is clicked.
   c) When the form is clicked.
   d) When the macro is double-clicked.

3. **To which event should the macro be attached?**
   a) The Before Update event
   b) The On Delete event
   c) The On Click event
   d) The On Close event

4. **Attach the macro to the On Click event of the button.**

   a. In the cmdContact command button Property Sheet pane, **select the Event tab.**

   b. From the On Click drop-down list, **select mcrMyContact.**

   c. **Close the Property Sheet pane.**

   d. **Save the form as *frmMyCustomerData***

   e. **Open the form in Form view and click Contact** to test the macro.

   f. Observe that the Contact form for that customer number is displayed.

   g. **Close the form window.**

TOPIC C
Restrict Records Using a Condition

You have automated the task of opening a form by adding a command button to the form and attaching the macro to it. Now, you would like to refine the output of the macro further. In this topic, you will restrict records using a condition in a macro.

Merely adding a macro to a database application and attaching it to a form does not always produce the result you desire. A macro designed to open a form displaying customer contact information may not show information related to the customer you need to contact and therefore does not serve its purpose. By restricting records using expressions and operators, you will ensure that the macro produces the desired results.

Macro Conditions

Definition:

A *macro condition* is an expression that enables a macro to perform certain tasks only if a specific situation exists. When you use a condition, the macro will perform a defined set of tasks depending on whether the expression returns a value that is True or False. When the expression returns a value that is True, all the actions are performed, and when the expression returns a False value, none of the actions are performed. Conditions can be entered in the Condition column of the Macro Builder window. A single condition can control more than one action.

Example:

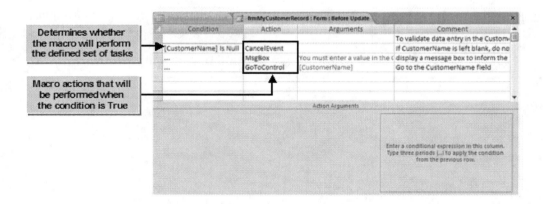

The Where Condition

The *Where condition* filters and selects the records in reports or forms and their underlying tables or queries. This condition is applicable as an argument for the macro actions OpenForm and OpenReport. The Where condition field appears in the Action Arguments pane for these macro actions. For example, the Where condition specified for an OpenForm action can be used to compare and display matching records from two related forms.

How to Restrict Records Using a Condition

Procedure Reference: Restrict Records Using a Where Condition

To restrict records using a Where condition:

1. In the Property Sheet pane, select the Event tab.
2. Click the Build button in the text box of the event to which the macro will be attached.
3. Select the Macro Builder window and click OK.
4. In the Macro Builder window, select the Open Form action.
5. In the Action Arguments pane for the Open Form action, enter the arguments.
   a. From the Form Name text box's drop-down list, select the form that is to be displayed.
   b. In the Where Condition text box, click the Build button so that the Expression Builder dialog box is displayed.
   c. In the Expression Builder dialog box, build the desired expression by adding operators and field names.
6. Save the macro.
7. Close the Property Sheet pane and the Macro Builder window.
8. Test the macro by executing the event, which will trigger the macro.

ACTIVITY 3-3

Entering an Expression in a Macro Argument

Data Files:

Macro.accdb

Before You Begin:

If necessary, from the C:\084889Data\Macros folder, open the Macro.accdb file.

Scenario:

The macro you are working on does not work the way you had planned. When you use the macro to open the Contact form, the record displayed is not in sync with the record in the frmMyCustomerData form. You know that by using a Where condition, you can improve this macro.

What You Do	How You Do It
1. Open the Macro Builder window for the command button's On Click event.	a. **Open the frmMyCustomerData form in Design view.**
	b. On the Design contextual tab, in the Tools group, **click Property Sheet.**
	c. In the Property Sheet pane, **verify that the Event tab is selected.**
	d. On the Event page, **click the On Click event's Build button.**
	e. Observe that the Choose Builder window is displayed. **Click OK.**

2. **Enter the Where Condition expression using the Expression Builder dialog box.**

a. In the Action column, **select the OpenForm entry** so that the Action Arguments pane for the action is displayed.

b. In the Action Arguments pane, **click in the Where Condition text box and then click the Build button** to launch the Expression Builder dialog box.

c. In the Expression Builder dialog box, in the list box on the left, **double-click the Forms folder** to expand it.

d. **Double-click the All Forms folder** to display all the forms in the selected folder.

e. **Click the frmMyCustomerData folder** so that the elements within the folder are displayed.

f. In the Expression Builder dialog box, in the Expression text area, **type [CustomerNum]**

g. **Click the Equal To (=) operator button** to display the operator in the Expression text area.

h. In the Expression Builder dialog box, in the list box at the center, **double-click the CustomerNum field** to display the expression in the Expression text area.

i. **Click OK** to close the Expression Builder dialog box.

3. **Test the command button.**

a. **Click the Save button.**

b. **Close the Macro Builder window.**

c. **View frmMyCustomerData in Form view.**

d. **Advance to record 2.**

e. **Verify that the customer number for this record is 185 and click Contact.**

f. Observe that the customer number displayed in the frmContact form matches that in the frmCustomerData form.

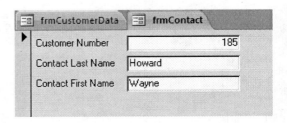

g. **Save and close the form windows.**

h. **Close the database.**

TOPIC D
Validate Data Using a Macro

You know how to build a basic macro and you are now ready to create more advanced macros. You need to ensure the accuracy of the data being entered in your database and inform users when they make an error while entering data. In this topic, you will use a macro to validate data entry and display appropriate alert messages to the user in case of an error.

If your database application is being used for data entry, you want to ensure the quality of the data being entered. It can be frustrating if you are not able to find the address of a customer to whom you need to send a package. Creating a macro to validate the data entry process will prompt the user to complete entering vital information. This, in turn, will benefit the user and ensure data integrity.

Event Properties for Data Validation

There are some common event properties that are used to trigger data validation.

Event Property	When the Macro Will Execute
Before Update	Before the entered data is updated.
After Update	After the entered data is updated.
Before Insert	After you type in a new record.
On Delete	In response to a deletion request, but before the record is deleted.

Macro Actions for Data Validation

When validating data, the macro is likely to contain certain macro actions.

Action	Use Action To
Cancel Event	Prevent a user from posting a new record unless certain conditions are met.
GoToControl	Specify where on the form the insertion point is to be placed.
MsgBox	Display a custom message box.

Planning for a Macro

Before actually creating a macro, you should plan what it will do. When planning for a macro you need to follow a set of guidelines.

Guidelines

- What action by the user will trigger the macro?
- What is the first thing the macro will do? The second?
- Which control will trigger the macro?
- Which event property will trigger the macro?
- When will you want this macro to run?

Example:

The figure shows a flow chart illustrating the plan for a macro. Drawing a flow chart can help make your plan clear and easy to follow. For example, you can create a macro in a Customer Details form that will not allow the user to save records when the CustomerName field is left blank. You can also add a macro action to alert the user with a message box. Finally, the insertion point can be moved to the CustomerName field to enable the user to fill in the blank field.

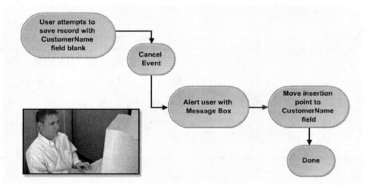

Figure 3-3: A flow chart plan for a macro.

Functionality of Macros

Typically, macros on forms can be grouped into categories according to their function. The macros in each category contain unique constructions that enable them to perform the indicated tasks.

- Validating data: You can create a macro to ensure that data entry is mandatory in a field or in order to display a custom dialog box that prompts the user for additional information.

- Setting values: A powerful use for macros in a form is to have a macro set values for a control, field, or property. This can make data entry easier and more accurate.

- Navigating between forms and records: You can create a macro that moves to a specific control, record, or page in a form.

- Filtering, finding, and printing records: You can create macros to automate the processes of filtering, finding, and printing records. A custom dialog box can be displayed to initiate the process specific to the user's needs.

Embedded Macros

Definition:

Embedded macros are macros that are part of an event property. They can be accessed only from the event property of the object they are attached to and cannot be accessed from the Navigation pane like regular macros. Embedded macros can be attached to the event property of a form, report, or control.

Example:

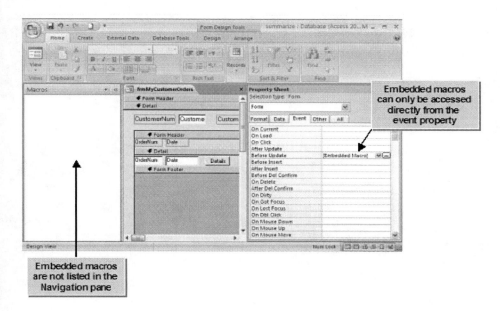

Embedded macros can only be accessed directly from the event property

Embedded macros are not listed in the Navigation pane

How to Validate Data Using a Macro

Procedure Reference: Make Data Entry Mandatory Using a Macro

To make data entry mandatory using a macro:

1. Open the form in Design view.
2. In the form, in the Before Update property box, open the Macro builder.
3. Open the Condition column.
4. Create an Is Null condition for the appropriate field to make data entry in the field mandatory.
5. Create a CancelEvent action to prevent the user from saving the record with invalid data.
6. Save the macro.

Procedure Reference: Modify an Existing Macro to Display a Message Box

To modify an existing macro to display a message box:

1. Open the existing macro in Design view.
2. Insert a new row in the macro.
3. In the Action column of the new row, click the drop-down arrow and select MsgBox.
4. In the Action Arguments pane, add message text, select a message type, and enter a title for the message box.
5. Add comments in the Comment column of the Macro Builder window.

6. Save your changes.

ACTIVITY 3-4
Making Data Entry Mandatory Using a Macro

Data Files:

Interaction.accdb

Before You Begin:

From the C:\084889Data\Macros folder, open the Interaction.accdb file.

Scenario:

You have planned a macro to validate data entry in a field and now you need to build it. The macro you want to create will not allow a record to be saved without data in the CustomerName field. It will also return the insertion point to this field if an attempt to save is made and the field is blank.

What You Do	How You Do It
1. Open the frmCustomerRecord form in Design view.	a. Open the frmCustomerRecord form in Design view.
	b. Verify that the Property Sheet pane for the form is displayed.
2. Open the Macro Builder window from the Before Update event.	a. If necessary, in the Property Sheet pane, **select the Event tab.**
	b. **Select the Before Update event and click the Build button** so that the Choose Builder window is displayed.
	c. In the Choose Builder dialog box, **verify that Macro Builder is selected and click OK.**
3. Enter the conditions in the macro.	a. On the Design contextual tab, in the Show/Hide group, **click Conditions.**
	b. In the first row of the Condition column, **type *[CustomerName] Is Null***

4. **Add an action to prevent a record from being saved in case of a blank field.**

   a. In the first row of the Action column, **click the drop-down arrow and select CancelEvent** to prevent the user from saving a record when there are blank fields in it.

   b. In the first row of the Comment column, **type *If CustomerName is left blank, do not save the record***

5. **Add a macro action to move the insertion point to the Customer Name field that is left blank.**

   a. In the second row of the Condition column, **type ...** so that you can attach multiple actions to one condition.

   b. In the second row of the Action column, **click the drop-down arrow and select GoToControl** to move the insertion point to the blank field.

   c. In the Action Arguments pane, in the Control Name text box, **type [CustomerName]**

   d. In the second row of the Comment column, **type *Go to the CustomerName field***

6. **Save the macro and the form.**

   a. **Click the Save button and close the Macro Builder window.**

   b. Observe that the macro is attached to the Before Update property.

   c. **Close the form's Property Sheet pane.**

   d. **Save the form as *frmMyCustomer-Record***

7. **Test the macro by trying to enter a new record.**

   a. **Open frmMyCustomerRecord in Form view**, and on the Home tab, in the Records group, **click New** to begin a new record.

   b. In the Customer Number field, **type *303* and press Tab twice** to leave the CustomerName field blank.

   c. **Enter the following data for the remaining fields:**

      Address: 15 West Avenue

      City: Toronto

      Region: Ontario

      Country: Canada

      Postal Code: J2D 4T1

      Phone: 7855555734

      Fax: 7855555225

   d. On the Home tab, in the Records group, **click Save.**

   e. Observe that you are unable to save the new record and the record you entered is still displayed with the pencil icon showing on the left. The insertion point is in the CustomerName field. Because the condition is True (the field is empty), the macro carried out the macro actions.

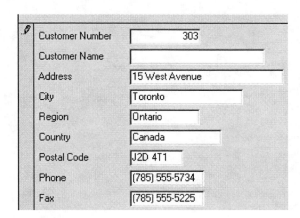

   f. **Close the form.**

   g. **Try to save the new record.** Observe that a dialog box appears to indicate that you will not be able to save the new record. Since there is no value in the CustomerName field, Access prevents the user from saving the record.

h. In the Microsoft Office Access message box, **click Yes.**

ACTIVITY 3-5

Modifying a Macro to Display a Message Box

Data Files:

Interaction.accdb

Before You Begin:

If necessary, from the C:\084889Data\Macros folder, open the Interaction.accdb file.

Scenario:

After testing your macro to validate data entry, you feel that it would be better to inform users why they are not able to save the record. With an appropriate alert message, users will know where they have made a mistake when entering data and can correct it.

What You Do	How You Do It
1. Open the embedded macro in the frmMyCustomerRecord form.	a. **Open frmMyCustomerRecord in Design view.**
	b. On the Design contextual tab, in the Tools group, **click Property Sheet.**
	c. **Verify that the Event tab is selected.**
	d. In the Property Sheet pane, **click the Build button for the Before Update event** to open the Macro Builder window.

2. **Attach another action to the macro condition.**

a. In the Macro Builder window, in the second row, **right-click the Selector tab** to display the shortcut menu.

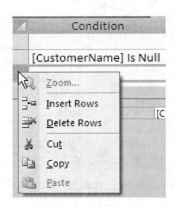

b. From the shortcut menu, **choose Insert Rows.**

c. In the Condition column of the new row, **type ...**

d. In the Action column of the new row, from the drop-down list, **select MsgBox.**

3. **Enter the message in the Action Arguments pane.**

a. In the Action Arguments pane, in the Message text box, **type *You must enter a value in the CustomerName field***

b. In the Type text box, **click,** and from the drop-down list, **select Information** to display the information icon for the message box.

c. In the Title text box, **type *Validate Data*** as the title for the message box.

4. **Add a comment for the MsgBox action.**

a. In the Comment column of the new row, **type ... *display a message box to inform the user why the record is not saved***

b. **Save your changes and close the Macro Builder window.**

c. **Switch to Form view,** and on the Home tab, in the Records group, **click New.**

d. In the Customer Number field, **type *303* and press Tab twice** to leave the CustomerName field blank.

e. **Enter the following data for the remaining fields:**

      Address: 15 West Avenue

      City: Toronto

      Region: Ontario

      Country: Canada

      Postal Code: J2D 4T1

      Phone: 7855555732

      Fax: 7855555226

f. On the Home tab, in the Records group, **click Save.**

g. Observe that a message box appears, prompting you to fill in the customer name.

h. **Click OK.**

i. **Close the form.**

j. **Click OK and then click Yes.**

TOPIC E
Automate Data Entry Using a Macro

You learned to use macros to validate data entry and interact with database users. You can also use macros to avoid errors and save time during data entry by automating the data entry process. Instead of having users type in the same data over and over for each record with the possibility of invalid data being entered, a macro can automate the entry of information. In this topic, you will use macros to automate parts of the data-entry process.

Suppose you wanted to run a report that showed a listing of all customers in the state of California. Simple errors in data entry can have an impact on the accuracy of your reports. Automating data entry can help ensure the quality of your data. For example, you could create a macro that automatically enters the country name based on the region entered. As a benefit to database users, this automation also saves data-entry time.

Event Properties for Automating Data Entry

An event property is the name by which an event is referred. The event property determines when the macro attached to it will be executed. For example, the event property On Enter determines that the macro will be executed when the user arrives on a control.

Event Property	When the Macro Will Be Executed
On Enter	Upon arriving on a control, but before the control has focus.
Before Update	Before the control data is updated.
After Update	After the changed control data is updated.
On Exit	Upon leaving a control, but before the focus is removed.

Macro Actions for Automating Data Entry

When you intend to set values to a macro for automating the data entry process, it is likely that you will use macro actions.

Action	Description
SetValue	Used to enter a value automatically in a field. The field name and the value that needs to be entered in the field are mentioned as arguments. You need to enter the arguments in the Action Arguments pane for this action.
GoToControl	Used to specify the field where the insertion point needs to be moved after a value.

How to Automate Data Entry Using a Macro

Procedure Reference: Specify a Condition for Automating Data Entry

To specify a condition for automating data entry:

1. Open the form in which you need to create the macro.

2. Select a field to which you want to attach the condition.

3. In the Property Sheet pane, select the appropriate event that should trigger the macro.

4. Open the Macro Builder window.

5. Click the Conditions button to make the Condition column visible.

6. Apply the appropriate conditions to automate data entry for the specified field.

7. In the Macro Builder window, from the Actions column drop-down list, select SetValue to automatically enter the specified value in the chosen field.

8. In another row of the Action column, select GoToControl to move the insertion point to the specified field after the data is entered.

9. Test the macro.

ACTIVITY 3-6
Creating a Macro that Will Automate Data Entry

Data Files:

Interaction.accdb

Before You Begin:

If necessary, from the C:\084889Data\Macros folder, open the Interaction.accdb file.

Scenario:

The customer service manager is thrilled with the macros you have created to remind data entry representatives to input customer names. Now that she sees the potential of macros, she has another request. She would like you to create a macro that will automatically input Canada in the Country Name field if Alberta or Ontario is entered into the Region field and then move the insertion point to the next field.

What You Do	How You Do It
1. Create an embedded macro in the form frmMyCustomerRecord.	a. **Open the frmMyCustomerRecord form in Design view.**
	b. **Select the Region text box,** and in the Tools group, **click Property Sheet.**
	c. On the Event page, **select the On Exit event and click the Build button** to display the Choose Builder window.
	d. In the Choose Builder dialog box, **verify that Macro Builder is selected and click OK.**

<table>
<tr>
<td>

2. **Add the SetValue action to automatically enter Canada when either Alberta or Ontario is entered in the region field.**

</td>
<td>

a. On the Design contextual tab, in the Show/Hide group, **click Conditions.**

b. On the Design contextual tab, in the Show/Hide group, **click Show All Actions** so that all the macro actions are available for selection.

c. In the first row of the Condition column, **type *[Region] In ("Alberta","Ontario")***

d. In the first row of the Action column, from the drop-down list, **select SetValue.**

e. In the Action Arguments pane of the Set Value action, **enter the following:**
   - **Item:** [Country]
   - **Expression:** "Canada"

f. In the first row of the Comment column, **type *If Region is Alberta or Ontario, set Country to Canada***

</td>
</tr>
<tr>
<td>

3. **Add the GoToControl action to move the insertion point to another field.**

</td>
<td>

a. In the second row of the Condition column, **type ...** to indicate that you would like to attach another action to the original condition.

b. In the second row of the Action column, from the drop-down list, **select GoToControl** to move the insertion point to another field.

c. In the Action Arguments pane, in the Control Name text box, **type *[PostalCode]*** to specify to which field you want the insertion point to move.

d. In the second row of the Comment column, **type *...go to the PostalCode field***

e. **Save and close the Macro Builder window.**

</td>
</tr>
</table>

f. Observe that the Property Sheet pane shows the new macro, which has been embedded in the Region field's On Exit event.

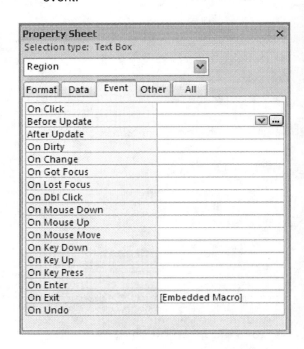

g. **Close the Property Sheet pane.**

4. **Test the macro in Form view by entering a new record.**

a. In Form view, **click the New Record button.**

b. **Enter the following values:**
    Customer Number: 367
    Customer Name: The Hitching Rail
    Address: 455 Creek Rd.
    City: Huntsville
    Region: Ontario

c. **Press Tab.**

d. Observe that when Ontario is entered in the Region field, the value Canada is automatically entered into the Country field, and the insertion point moves to the Postal Code field.

e. **Complete the form with the following values:**

> **Postal Code:** THX138
>
> **Phone:** 7875555895
>
> **Fax:** 7875555856

f. **Click Save** to save the new record.

g. **Close the database.**

Lesson 3 Follow-up

In this lesson, you simplified tasks, added interaction, and validated data by creating and revising macros.

1. **How might restricting records using a Where condition help you on the job?**

2. **How might validating data entry help when creating forms in the future?**

4 | Making Effective Use of Forms

Lesson Time: 1 hour(s), 10 minutes

Lesson Objectives:

In this lesson, you will display data more effectively in a form.

You will:

● Display a calendar in a form.

● Organize information using a tab control in a form.

● Display a summary of data in a form using a PivotChart and a PivotTable.

Introduction

Most databases provide forms for data entry and for viewing data. In this lesson, you will identify a few techniques that will help enhance the usability of your forms, and in turn, the productivity of the users of your database.

Most users of databases work with forms every day. As you learn more about the capabilities of forms, you will be able to build in more functionality, save user time and work, and also present data in a more organized way.

TOPIC A
Display a Calendar on a Form

You have used many different types of controls in your forms, but using simple controls will keep you from taking advantage of advanced tools. In this topic, you will display a calendar in a form.

When working closely with dates, having a calendar nearby is very helpful. Instead of using a paper calendar or switching to another program to check dates, you can include a calendar in your database forms.

ActiveX Controls

ActiveX controls are software components that are modeled on the Microsoft Component Object Model (COM). ActiveX controls are usually graphical objects that do not operate as standalone solutions, and they run only in the Windows environment. Common ActiveX controls include check boxes, text boxes, list boxes, option buttons, and command buttons.

Form Format Properties

A form has a number of format properties that can be set to control its appearance. There are some commonly used format properties, and the default setting for each property is indicated by an asterisk (*) in the following table.

Form Format Property	Settings
Default View	Single Form*, Continuous Forms, Datasheet, PivotTable, PivotChart
Scroll Bars	Neither, Horizontal Only, Vertical Only, Both*
Record Selectors	Yes*, No
Navigation Buttons	Yes*, No
Dividing Lines	Yes, No*
Border Style	None, Thin, Sizable*, Dialog
Control Box	Yes*, No
Min Max Buttons	None, Min Enabled, Max Enabled, Both Enabled*
Close Button	Yes*, No
Auto Center	Yes, No*

Border Style Settings

The Border Style property of a form contains the options that are described in the following table.

Setting	Description
None	Form has no border or border elements; not resizable

Setting	Description
Thin	Form has a thin border and can include any of the border elements; not resizable
Sizable	Form has the default border for Access forms and can include any of the border elements; resizable
Dialog	Form has a thick border and can only have a title bar, Close button, and Control box; not resizable

How to Display a Calendar in a Form

Procedure Reference: Add a Calendar Control to a Form

To add a Calendar control to a form:

1. Open the form in Design view.
2. On the Design contextual tab, in the Controls group, click the Insert ActiveX Control button.
3. In the Insert ActiveX Control dialog box, select the Calendar control you wish to add.
4. Use the Form Format properties to get the desired effect.
5. Format the Calendar control by setting its properties.
6. Create a macro to move the Calendar to a different position in the form.
7. Create a command button in the form from which the Calendar control is to be activated.
8. Attach the macro to the command button.
9. Test the command button as well as the macro.

ACTIVITY 4-1

Displaying a Calendar in a Form

Data Files:

Forms.accdb

Before You Begin:

From the C:\084889Data\EffectiveForms folder, open the Forms.accdb database.

Scenario:

You created the frmOrders form to be used for order entries. The supervisor of the customer service group tells you that the people taking orders often need to refer to a calendar to answer customer questions, such as when they will receive a shipment. A calendar is necessary so that the customer service employees can take weekends and holidays into account when they make an estimate as to when orders will be shipped.

What You Do	How You Do It
1. Place a Calendar Control 12.0 on a new form.	a. On the Create tab, in the Forms group, **click Blank Form.**
	b. **Close the Field List pane.**
	c. **Switch to Design view.**
	d. On the Design contextual tab, in the Controls group, **click the Insert ActiveX Control button** to display the Insert ActiveX Control dialog box.
	e. In the Insert ActiveX Control dialog box, **select Calendar Control 12.0 and click OK** to insert the control in the form.

2. Set the properties to format the form.

a. On the Design contextual tab, in the Tools group, **click Property Sheet** to display the Property Sheet pane.

b. In the Property Sheet pane, from the Selection Type drop-down list, **select Form.**

c. In the Property Sheet pane, **select the Format tab.**

d. In the Caption text box, **type *Lone Pine Calendar***

e. From the Auto Center drop-down list, **select Yes.**

f. From the Border Style drop-down list, **select Dialog.**

g. From the Record Selectors drop-down list, **select No** to set the Record Selectors property to No.

h. From the Navigation Buttons drop-down list, **select No** to disable the navigation buttons.

i. **Verify that the Dividing Lines property is set to No.**

j. From the Scroll Bars drop-down list, **select Neither.**

k. In the Property Sheet pane, on the Other tab, from the Pop Up drop-down list, **select Yes.**

l. **Close the Property Sheet pane.**

m. If necessary, **resize the form** to fit the control.

3. **Set the Calendar control proper-ties.**

    a. On the form, **click** to select Calendar Control, and on the Design contextual tab, in the Tools group, **click Property Sheet.**

    b. In the Property Sheet pane, **verify that the Other tab is selected,** and from the MonthLength drop-down list, **select English** to display the month fully instead of the shortened form.

    c. From the ValueIsNull drop-down list, **select Yes** to accept Null values.

    d. **Close the Property Sheet pane.**

    e. **Save the form as *frmMyCalendar* and close it.**

4. **Create a command button to access the Calendar control from the form.**

    a. **Open frmOrders in Design view.**

    b. On the Design contextual tab, in the Controls group, **select the Use Control Wizards button.**

    c. On the Design contextual tab, in the Controls group, **click Button and then click to the right of the OrderNum text box** to display the Command Button Wizard.

    d. In the Command Button Wizard, in the Categories list box, **select Form Opera-tions.**

    e. In the Actions list box, **select Open Form and click Next.**

    f. In the list box, **select frmMyCalendar and click Next.**

    g. **Select the Text option, press Tab, type *Show Calendar* and click Next.**

    h. **Type *cmdCalendar* and click Finish.**

    i. **Switch to Form view and click Show Calendar.**

j. Observe that the calendar is displayed when the Show Calendar command button is clicked.

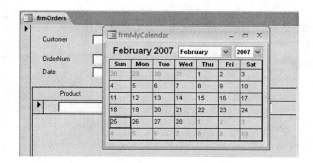

k. **Close the Lone Pine Calendar.**

l. **Save the form as *frmMyOrders* and close it.**

5. **Create a new macro to open the frmMyCalendar form.**

a. On the Create tab, in the Other group, **click Macro** to display the Macro Builder window.

b. In the first row of the Action column, from the drop-down list, **select OpenForm.**

c. In the Action Arguments pane, **click in the Form Name text box,** and from the drop-down list, **select frmMyCalendar.**

d. In the second row of the Action column, from the drop-down list, **select MoveSize,** and in the Action Argument pane, in the Right text box, **type *7*** to display the calendar to the right of the form.

e. **Save the macro as *mcrCalendar* and close it.**

6. Attach the macro to the command button.

a. **Display frmMyOrders in Design view and verify that the Show Calendar command button is selected.**

b. On the Design contextual tab, in the Tools group, **click Property Sheet.**

c. On the Event tab, in the On Click text box, from the drop-down list, **select mcrCalendar.**

d. **Save the form.**

e. **Switch to Form view and click Show Calendar.**

f. Observe that the Calendar is displayed to the right of the form.

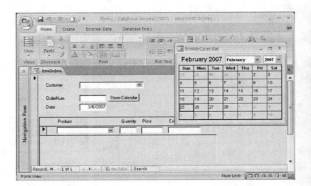

g. **Close the form window and the calendar window.**

TOPIC B
Organize Information with Tab Pages

You may have used boxes, lines, and other features to help draw the user's eye to certain groupings of data in forms. Another way to organize information in a form is to use tab pages. In this topic, you will use tab pages to create multiple pages in a single form.

Rather than having users open several different forms to view different sets of information, you can make their work more efficient by providing one form with tab pages. This enables you to place more data in a single form and allows users easier access to what they need.

The Tab Control

Definition:

A *Tab control* is an Access control that allows you to create multiple pages in one form. Each page is separated by its own tab and becomes active when the user selects a tab. You can use the same controls on a tab page that you would use when creating a single-page form.

Example:

How to Organize Information with Tab Pages

Procedure Reference: Create a New Form with Tab Pages

To create a new form with tab pages:

1. Create a new form in Design view.
2. Select the form and, in the Property Sheet pane, set the Record Source to the query or table.
3. On the Design contextual tab, in the Controls group, click the Tab Control button.
4. Select the form where you want to place the Tab control.
5. Set the Name property for each of the tabs.
6. Display the Field List pane and add the fields you want on each tab page.
7. Save the form.

ACTIVITY 4-2
Creating Tab Pages in a Form

Data Files:

Tab.accdb

Before You Begin:

From the C:\084889Data\EffectiveForms folder, open the Tab.accdb file.

Scenario:

In an informal chat with the manager of human resources, whose department also uses Access databases, you tell her about all the interesting things you have learned in Access that help increase efficiency and usability. She mentions that the HR department currently has a lot of different forms in its database, each with a special purpose, and wonders if there is a better way to handle data and avoid having to open and close so many forms. You reply that you have heard about Tab controls in forms and agree to build a new form for her to try out.

What You Do	How You Do It
1. Create a new form and add a Tab control to the form.	a. On the Create tab, in the Forms group, **click Blank Form** to create a new form.
	b. **Close the Field List pane and view the new form in Design view.**
	c. On the Design contextual tab, in the Tools group, **click Property Sheet** to display the Property Sheet pane.
	d. In the Property Sheet pane, **select the Data tab,** and from the Record Source drop-down list, **select qselEmployeeInfo.**
	e. On the Design contextual tab, in the Controls group, **click the Tab Control button.**
	f. In the form, in the 1-inch ruler position, **click at the intersection of the gridlines** to create the tab pages in the form.
	g. **Resize the tab control** so that the bottom edge of the control is in line with the 4-inch mark on the horizontal ruler.

2. **Add the fields related to personal details on the Page 1 tab.**

   a. On the Design contextual tab, in the Tools group, **click Add Existing Fields** to display the Field List pane.

   b. If necessary, **click Show Only Fields In The Current Record Source.**

   c. **Select Page 1 of the tab control.**

   d. In the Property Sheet pane, **select the Format tab.**

   e. In the Caption text box, **type *Personal***

   f. In the Field List pane, **drag the following fields to the Personal tab area in this order:**
      - EmployeeFirstName
      - EmployeeLastName
      - Street
      - City
      - State
      - ZipCode
      - HomePhone

3. **Add the fields related to company information on the Page 2 tab.**

   a. **Select Page 2 of the tab control.**

   b. If necessary, on the Design contextual tab, in the Tools group, **click Property Sheet.**

   c. In the Caption text box, **type *Company***

   d. On the Design contextual tab, in the Tools group, **click Add Existing Fields** to display the Field List pane.

e. In the Field List pane, **drag the following fields to the Company tab area:**

- EmployeeFirstName
- EmployeeLastName
- DeptNum
- DeptName
- OfficeExt
- HourlyRate
- WeeklyHours
- HealthIns

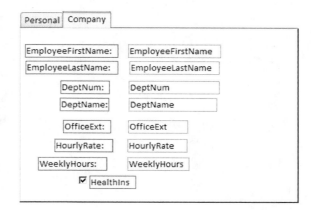

f. **Save the form as** *frmMyEmployeeInfo*

g. **Switch to Form view and test the tab pages.**

4. Change the settings of the tabs.

a. **Switch to Design view.**

b. **Select the Tab control.**

c. **Right-click the Tab control and choose Page Order.**

d. In the Page Order dialog box, **verify that Personal is selected.**

e. **Click Move Down and then click OK.**

f. Observe that the order of the Personal and Company tab pages has changed.

g. In the Property Sheet pane for the Tab control, on the Format tab, **click the Style drop-down arrow and select Buttons** to change the display of the tabs to the button style.

h. **Switch to Form view.**

i. Observe that the tabs are now appearing as buttons.

j. **Save and close the form.**

k. **Close the database.**

TOPIC C
Display a Summary of Data in a Form

You presented data in a form using tab pages. Presenting a summary of data can be very useful to users who access your database. You can create PivotCharts and PivotTables in forms to display a summary of data. In this topic, you will create a PivotChart and PivotTable.

PivotChart view or PivotTable view of a query is available to the user only after he or she opens the query and switches to that view. The advantage of creating a PivotChart or a PivotTable in a form is that it is immediately available when the form is opened.

The Subform Wizard

A *subform* is a form that is inserted into another form that enables you to view data from more than one table or query in the same form. The *Subform Wizard* is a tool used to create a new subform in a main form or embed an existing form into another.

How to Display a Summary of Data in a Form

Procedure Reference: Create a PivotChart in a Form

To create a PivotChart in a form:

1. Create a new form using the PivotChart Wizard based on a query.
2. In the Chart Field List pane, drag the appropriate fields to the Category, Series, and Data Fields areas in the PivotChart.
3. Display a legend.
4. Make any necessary changes to the horizontal Axis Title and vertical Axis Title.
5. Save and close the form.
6. Open the form in which the PivotChart will be displayed.
7. Create a subform control in the form using the Subform Wizard.
8. Adjust the size of the subform control.
9. Save and close the form.
10. Switch to Form view and observe the changes in the PivotChart as you move through the records.

Procedure Reference: Create a PivotTable in a Form

To create a PivotTable in a form:

1. Create a new form using the PivotTable Wizard based on a query.
2. In the PivotTable List pane, drag the appropriate fields to the Row, Column, and Totals or Detail Fields areas in the PivotTable.
3. Display a legend.
4. Make any necessary changes to the horizontal Axis Title and vertical Axis Title.
5. Save and close the form.
6. Open the form in which the PivotTable will be displayed.
7. Create a subform control in the form using the Subform Wizard.
8. Adjust the size of the subform control.

9. Save and close the form.

10. Switch to Form view and observe the changes in the PivotTable as you move through the records.

ACTIVITY 4-3

Creating a PivotChart in a Form

Data Files:

PivotChartForm.accdb

Before You Begin:

From the C:\084889Data\EffectiveForms folder, open the PivotChartForm.accdb database.

Scenario:

You think that a PivotChart is a very effective way to present data. Your customer service colleagues use a form you created to check on customers' orders. It might be helpful if they could easily see the purchase volume of customers for a certain number of months.

What You Do	How You Do It
1. Create a new form in PivotChart layout based on the fields in the qselCustExtended query.	a. On the Create tab, in the Forms group, **click PivotChart.**
	b. **Click the form** to display the Chart Field List pane.
	c. **Drag the Chart Field List pane** to the left of the Form window so that you have a clear view of the form.
	d. From the Chart Field List pane, **drag the CustomerName field to the Drop Category Fields Here area.**
	e. From the Chart Field List pane, **drag the Date By Month field to the Drop Series Fields Here area.**
	f. From the Chart Field List pane, **drag the ExtendedPrice field to the Drop Data Fields Here area.**
	g. Observe that the PivotChart is created.
	h. **Close the Chart Field List pane.**
2. Create a legend that displays the months Jan, Feb, and Mar.	a. In the Show/Hide group, **click Legend.**

b. Observe the legend that is displayed below the Years field button.

c. **Right-click the Years field button and choose Expand** so that the Quarters field button is displayed.

d. **Right-click the Quarters field button and choose Expand** so that the Months field button is displayed.

e. **Drag the Years field button off the form** to remove it.

f. **Drag the Quarters field button off the form** to remove it.

3. **Change the vertical Axis Title to Purchases and delete the horizontal Axis Title.**

a. **Select the vertical Axis Title** and on the Design contextual tab, in the Tools group, **click Property Sheet.**

b. In the Properties dialog box, on the Format tab, in the Caption text box, **change the caption to *Purchases***

c. **Close the Properties dialog box.**

d. **Select the horizontal Axis Title and press Delete.**

e. Observe that the Axis Title that was placed horizontally has been deleted from the chart.

f. On the Quick Access toolbar, **click the Save button,** and in the Save As dialog box, **type *frmMyPivotChart* and click OK.**

g. **Close frmMyPivotChart.**

4. **Create a subform in frmCustomerOrders using the Subform Wizard.**

a. In the Navigation pane, from the drop-down list, **select Forms** to display the forms.

b. **Open frmCustomerOrders in Design view.**

c. If necessary, on the Design contextual tab, in the Controls group, **click the Use Control Wizards button.**

d. On the Design contextual tab, in the Controls group, **click the Subform/ Subreport button.**

e. In the frmCustomerOrders form, **click below the CustomerName text box** to create a subform control and view the Subform Wizard.

f. On the Subform Wizard page, **select the Use An Existing Form option.**

g. **Observe that the frmMyPivotChart option is selected.**

h. **Click Next** to go to the next page of the wizard.

i. **Select the Define My Own option** to define the fields that link the subform to the main form.

j. In the Form/Report Fields section, from the first drop-down list, **select CustomerName.**

k. In the Subform/Subreport Fields section, from the first drop-down list, **select CustomerName.**

l. **Click Next** to go to the next page of the wizard.

m. **Click Finish** to complete the wizard and accept the default name for the subform.

5. **Save the form after making changes to the size of the subform control.**

a. **Resize the form, fields, and window of the subform control to their appropriate sizes.**

b. **Save the form as *frm-MyCustomerOrders***

c. **Switch to Form view.**

d. **Advance through the first four records** to view the PivotChart that displays a graphical summary of the data related to each record in the main form.

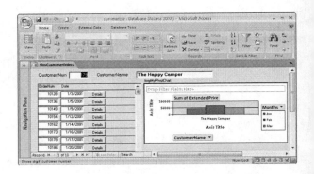

e. **Save and close the database.**

ACTIVITY 4-4

Creating a PivotTable in a Form

Data Files:

PivotTableForm.accdb

Before You Begin:

From the C:\084889Data\EffectiveForms folder, open the PivotTableForm.accdb database.

Scenario:

You realize that a PivotTable can be a very effective presentation of data. The customer service department uses a form you created to check on customers' orders. It might be helpful if they could also easily see the extended price at which a customer has made purchases over a period of three months.

What You Do	How You Do It
1. Create a new form in the Pivot-Table layout based on the fields in the qselCustExtended query.	a. On the Create tab, in the Forms group, **click the More Forms drop-down arrow and select PivotTable.**
	b. **Click the form** to display the PivotTable Field List pane.
	c. From the PivotTable Field List pane, **drag the CustomerName field to the Drop Row Fields Here area.**
	d. From the PivotTable Field List pane, **drag the Date By Month field to the Drop Column Fields Here area.**
	e. From the PivotTable Field List pane, **drag the ExtendedPrice field to the Drop Totals Or Detail Fields Here area.**
	f. Observe that the PivotTable is now populated with data.

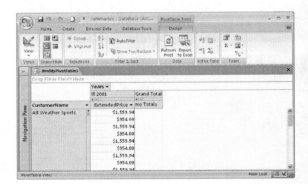

g. **Close the PivotTable Field List pane.**

2. **Expand the view of 2001 and Qtr1 and remove the Years and Quarters heading labels.**

a. **Expand the view of 2001** to display the first quarter.

b. **Expand Qtr1** to display the Jan, Feb, and Mar columns.

c. In the column heading area, **click Years and drag it to anywhere outside the table area, until an X appears.**

d. In the column heading area, **click Quarters and drag it out of the window until an X appears** to remove the Qtr1 field.

e. On the Quick Access toolbar, **click the Save button,** and in the Save As dialog box, **type *frmMyPivotTable* and click OK.**

f. **Close the frmMyPivotTable form.**

3. **Create a subform in frmCustomerOrders using the Subform Wizard.**

   a. In the Navigation pane, from the drop-down list, **select Forms** to display the forms.

   b. **Open frmCustomerOrders in Design view.**

   c. On the Design contextual tab, in the Controls group, **verify that the Use Control Wizards button is selected.**

   d. On the Design contextual tab, in the Controls group, **click the Subform/ Subreport button.**

   e. **In the frmCustomerOrders form, click below the CustomerName text box** to create a subform control and view the Subform Wizard.

   f. On the Subform Wizard page, **select the Use An Existing Form option.**

   g. Observe that the frmMyPivotTable option is selected.

   h. **Click Next** to go to the next page of the wizard.

   i. **Select the Define My Own option** to define the fields that link the subform to the main form.

   j. In the Form/Report Fields section, from the first drop-down list, **select CustomerName.**

   k. In the Subform/Subreport Fields section, from the first drop-down list, **select CustomerName.**

   l. **Click Next** to go to the next page of the wizard.

   m. **Click Finish** to complete the wizard and accept the default name for the subform.

4. **Save the form after making changes to the size of the subform control.**

   a. **Resize the form, fields, and window of the subform control to their appropriate sizes.**

   b. **Save the form.**

   c. **Switch to Form view.**

d. **Advance through the first four records**
to view how the PivotTable summarizes
the data related to the records in the main
form.

e. **Close the form window and the
database.**

Lesson 4 Follow-up

In this lesson, you made effective use of forms. The more functionality you build into your forms, the more time will be saved by the users of your database.

1. **Are there places in any of your existing databases where tab pages might be useful? Explain and give examples.**

2. **How can displaying a summary of data in your forms help end users of your database?**

5 Making Reports More Effective

Lesson Time: 45 minutes

Lesson Objectives:

In this lesson, you will customize reports by using various Microsoft® Office Access™ 2007 features, making them more effective.

You will:

- Add a chart to a report to increase its visual impact.

- Create a multiple-column report that uses functions and operators to control the printing of data.

- Create a macro that cancels the printing of a blank report.

- Create a snapshot of a report so that it can be viewed without the Access program.

Introduction

You already learned to write advanced queries and create customized forms. Similarly, reports can be customized to make them more effective. In this lesson, you will customize your reports.

Reports are your way of communicating database information throughout your company. By customizing reports, you can present your information in the most effective format to your employees. A customized report developed by using Access tools can reach a wider audience and enable you to get your message across in a more powerful way.

TOPIC A
Include a Chart in a Report

You have created a lot of reports and you saw how a PivotChart can be used on a form. Through its interactive feature, a PivotChart makes it possible to view data in different ways, depending on changes made to the form layout. However, you may not always need the interactivity of a PivotChart. In those instances, a standard chart would be useful. In this topic, you will include a chart in a report using Access tools.

Printed reports may be all the evidence that some users see of all your hard work with databases. Making those reports appear professional will enhance the impression that they make. Data that is represented graphically can also be easier to understand. By adding a chart, you can provide a visual overview of the data in the report.

Charts

Definition:

A *chart* is a graphical representation of information used to illustrate quantitative relationships. It is a diagram that depicts a relationship, often functional, between two sets of numbers or between a set of numbers and a set of categories. The values are often represented as a set of points having coordinates determined by the relationship. In such cases, the relationship between certain quantities are then plotted with reference to a set of axes.

Example:

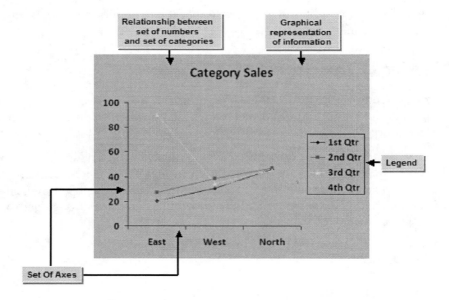

Chart Types

You can use the Chart Wizard to create charts from selected fields in tables or queries and also generate different types of charts. The varied purposes of reports, and the data found in them, determine the best choice of chart to use. Of the different chart types, the following table describes the most prominently used types.

Chart Type	Purpose
Column Chart	Used to compare multiple values of categories or differences over a period of time. The horizontal axis depicts categories and the vertical axis depicts values.
Bar Chart	Used for the same purposes as a Column Chart. However, the horizontal axis of a Bar Chart shows values and the vertical axis shows categories or periods of time.
Area Chart	Used to emphasize differences in individual values to the total over a period of time.
Line Chart	Used to compare trends over a period of time.
Pie Chart	Used to show the relationship of a part to the whole. It is suitable for depicting one data series or data at a point in time.

How to Include a Chart in a Report

Procedure Reference: Add a Chart to a Report Using the Chart Wizard

To add a chart to a report using the Chart Wizard:

1. Open the report in Design view.
2. On the Design contextual tab, in the Controls group, click the Insert Chart button.
3. In the report, click in the location where you want to insert a chart and start the Chart Wizard.
4. In the Chart Wizard, select the data source for the chart and click Next.
5. Select the fields that you want to include in the chart and click Next.
6. Select the chart type and click Next.
7. Click Preview Chart to get a sample preview of the chart.
8. Close the sample preview.
9. If desired, click Back to change the chart type. Select an appropriate chart type and click Next.
10. If necessary, drag and drop field buttons to the sample chart for the desired layout of data in the chart. Click Next.
11. Select fields that link the report and the chart only if you want the chart to change from record to record.
12. From the Report Fields and Chart Fields drop-down lists, select No Field if you want the chart to remain unchanged. Click Next.
13. Type a title for the chart and click Finish.
14. Format the chart.
    - If necessary, open the Property Sheet to format the chart.

- In the Width row, increase the width of the chart.

- In the Back Color row, click the drop-down arrow or the Build button to select a background color for the chart.

- In the Special Effect row, click the drop-down arrow to select a desired effect for your chart.

- In the Gridline Color row, click the drop-down arrow or the Build button to select the gridline color.

- Or, right-click the chart and from the shortcut menu, choose the color and effects to format the chart. You can also select Properties to apply different formatting to the chart in the Property Sheet pane.

15. Save the report.

ACTIVITY 5-1

Adding a Chart to a Report

Data Files:

Reports.accdb

Before You Begin:

From the C:\084889Data\Making Reports More Effective folder, open the Reports.accdb file.

Scenario:

You have created a summary report based on a query. The report shows the first quarter's total sales for each product in each category, total sales for each category, and a grand total. You would like to compare the sales in each category by adding a diagrammatic representation to the report. You need the visual representation to show only the total for each category.

What You Do	How You Do It
1. Preview the rptQ1CategorySales report in Design view.	a. **Open rptQ1CategorySales.**
	b. **Click the Next Page button** to advance to the next page.
	c. **Switch to Design view.**

2. Insert a chart in the Report footer to graphically represent sales for each category in the report.

a. If necessary, **close the Property Sheet pane.**

b. **Resize the Report footer** to accommodate the chart.

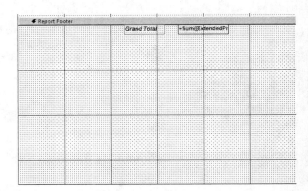

c. On the Design contextual tab, in the Controls group, **click the Insert Chart button.**

d. In the Report footer, **click in the first square** to create a chart control.

e. In the Chart Wizard, **select the Queries option,** and from the list of queries, **select Query: qtotCategories**.

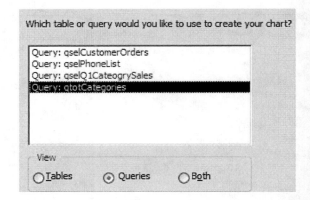

f. **Click Next.**

g. In the Chart Wizard, **click the >> button** to add the Category and Total Sales fields from the Available Fields list to the Fields For Chart list.

h. **Click Next.**

i. In the thumbnails of the chart types, **verify that Column Chart is selected and click Next**.

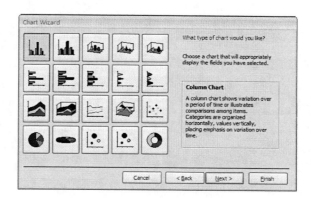

j. **Click Preview Chart** to examine the chart before it is created.

k. Notice that Column Chart is not the ideal choice for depicting the comparison of sales in each category at a point in time.

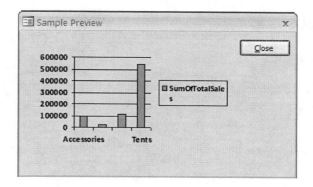

l. **Close the preview chart and click Back**.

m. From the thumbnails of the chart types, in the fourth row, in the first column, **select Pie Chart and click Next**.

n. **Click Preview Chart**.

o. Notice that the pie chart illustrates the categories in proportion to the total items.

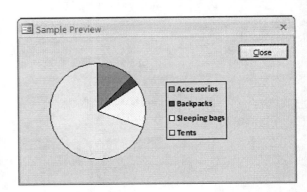

p. **Close the preview chart and click Next.**

q. From the first Report Fields drop-down list and the first Chart Fields drop-down list, **select No Field**.

r. **Click Next**.

s. In the text box for the chart title, **type *Q1 Category Sales* and click Finish**.

t. If necessary, **scroll down** to view the placeholder for the chart.

3. **Apply a background color to the chart.**

a. On the Design contextual tab, in the Tools group, **click Property Sheet**.

b. In the Property Sheet pane, on the Format tab, **click in the Back Color row** to view the Build button and then **click the Build button.**

c. In the Standard Colors section, in the fifth row, in the last column, **select the Brown 4 color.**

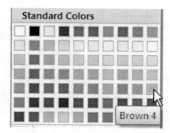

d. **Close the Property Sheet pane.**

e. Notice the change in the background color of the chart.

f. **Preview the report and view the chart on the second page.**

g. **Save the report as *rptMyQ1CategorySalesReport* and close it.**

h. **Close the database.**

TOPIC B
Print Data in Columns

You added a chart to a report to provide a clear, visual representation of data. You may also have reports that have many records, but with only one or two data fields each. In this topic, you will arrange your fields of data in multiple columns on the page.

Some of your reports may involve long lists of just a few fields of data—such as a phone or product list. These may be best arranged in multiple columns for readability.

String Concatenation Formulas

Concatenation is the operation of joining two character strings end to end. A string concatenation formula involves a binary operation usually accomplished by putting a concatenation operator between two strings. In Access, this operator is the ampersand (&) character. It helps to join character strings from several fields together into another destination field. A formula may sometimes consist of a text string. In such cases, the strings must be enclosed in double quotes.

How to Print Data in Columns
Procedure Reference: Create a Multiple-Column Report

To create a multiple-column report:

1. Create a new report in Design view.
2. Place the controls you want to print in each column in your chosen width in the Detail section.
3. Add a group header and/or footer.
4. Select the Page Setup contextual tab.
5. Open the Page Setup dialog box.
    *   In the Page Layout group, click the Columns button.
    *   In the Page Layout group, click Page Setup.
    *   Or, in the Page Layout group, click the Dialog Box Launcher.
6. In the Page Setup dialog box, select the Columns tab.
7. On the Columns tab, in the Grid Settings section, type the number of columns and column spacing.
8. In the Column Size section, type the column width and the column height.
9. In the Column Layout section, select the column layout.
10. Click OK to close the Page Setup dialog box.
11. Switch to Print Preview view to preview the report.
12. If necessary, in the Print group, click Print to launch the Print dialog box to print the report.
13. If necessary, save the report.

ACTIVITY 5-2

Printing Data in Columns

Data Files:

Print.accdb

Before You Begin:

From the C:\084889Data\Making Reports More Effective folder, open the Print.accdb file.

Scenario:

You have been asked to produce an internal phone list from your company's Human Resources database. You would like it to be easy to read with a divider for easy reference. You also want it to fit on one page so that people can post it on the wall near their phones. You have already created a query that extracts a few fields and puts the records in alphabetical order; this should be a good starting point.

What You Do	How You Do It
1. In the Print database, **create a new report in Design view and add a Label control**.	a. **Create a new report in Design view.**
	b. **Open the Property Sheet pane,** and in the Property Sheet pane, **select the Data tab**, and from the Record Source drop-down list, **select qselPhoneList**.

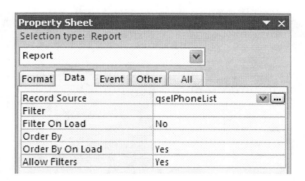

	c. **Close the Property Sheet pane**.
	d. On the Design contextual tab, and in the Controls group, **select the Label (Form Control) tool**.

e. In the Page Header section, at the top-left corner of the first square, **click** to create a Label control.

f. **Type *LonePineSales Internal Phone List***

g. In the Property Sheet pane, on the Format tab, **change the font size to 24**.

h. **Adjust the bars** to view the Page Header text.

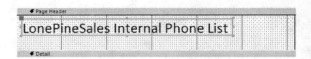

---

2. **In the Detail section, add a control that will print names in a desired format and add the OfficeExt field.**

a. In the Detail section, to the left of the first square, **add a Text Box control and delete its associated label**.

b. **Select the Text Box control,** and in the Property Sheet pane, on the Data tab, in the Control Source property text box, **type =[EmployeeLastName]&", "&[EmployeeFirstName]** to retrieve the employee names from qselPhoneList in order to display them in the text box.

 Right-click the Control Source property text box and choose Zoom to verify if the expression has been typed correctly.

c. **Close the Property Sheet pane.**

d. On the Design contextual tab, in the Tools group, **select Add Existing Fields** to open the Field List pane.

e. In the Field List pane, **click and drag the OfficeExt field next to the Text Box control in the Detail section and delete its associated label.**

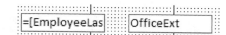

f. **Close the Field List pane.**

3. **Add a group header for the employee last name using the expression that will extract the first letter of each last name and set the appropriate group properties.**

a. On the Design contextual tab, in the Grouping & Totals group, **click Group & Sort** and in the Group, Sort, And Total pane, **click Add A Group.**

b. In the Select Field list, **click Expression.**

c. In the Expression Builder dialog box, in the Expression text area, **type =Left([EmployeeLastName],1) and copy the expression to the clipboard and click OK.**

d. Observe that the EmployeeLastName Header appears in the report.

e. In the Group, Sort, And Total pane, **click More.**

f. In the Group, Sort, And Total pane, for the grouping expression, in the With/Without A Header section, observe that the With A Header Section option is selected.

g. For the expression, from the Do Not Keep Group Together On One Page drop-down list, **select Keep Whole Group Together On One Page.**

h. **Close the Group, Sort, And Total pane.**

4. **Add a Text Box control to the left of the group header and paste the contents from the clipboard.**

   a. In the group header section, at the top-left corner of the first square, **add a Text Box control and delete its associated label**.

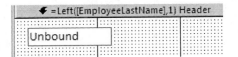

   b. In the group header section, **select the text box and display the Property Sheet pane**.

   c. In the Property Sheet pane, on the Data tab, in the Control Source text box, **paste the expression from the clipboard**.

   d. On the Format tab, from the Font Size drop-down list, **choose 10**.

5. **Adjust the column properties for the report and preview it.**

   a. On the Page Setup contextual tab, in the Page Layout group, **click the Dialog Box Launcher button** to open the Page Setup dialog box.

   b. In the Page Setup dialog box, on the Columns tab, in the Grid Settings section, **set Number Of Columns to *2* and set Column Spacing to *0.5***

Grid Settings	
Number of Columns:	2
Row Spacing:	0"
Column Spacing:	0.5"

   c. In the Column Size section, **uncheck the Same As Detail check box** to set a custom property and **type a width of *3* and a height of *2***

d. In the Column Layout section, **select the Down, Then Across option.**

e. **Click OK** to close the Page Setup dialog box.

f. **Close the Property Sheet pane.**

g. **Drag the Page Footer bar up so that it is directly below the Detail section text boxes.**

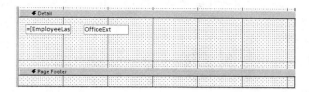

h. **Preview the report.**

i. **Verify that the names and phone extensions appear in two columns, and that the records are grouped by the first letter of the last name.**

j. If necessary, **print the report.**

k. **Save the report as *myPhoneList* and close it.**

l. **Close the database.**

TOPIC C
Cancel Printing of a Blank Report

You have been improving the visual appeal of your reports by adding charts and printing multiple columns. These are both cases where you have ample data to convey in your reports. But, sometimes the opposite situation will occur. In this topic, you will cancel the printing of a blank report.

If a report contains no records, the detail area of the report will be blank. While you do a bulk print of multiple reports, you might not have the time to open and check each report to see if it is blank or not. By using a macro to cancel printing of a blank report, you can save resources and time.

Report Events

You can use report events to run macros. Each report event has a specific property.

Event Property	Purpose
On Open	To open a custom dialog box for collecting report criteria before a report is previewed, printed, or the underlying query is run.
On Close	To display a menu or a switchboard form when the report window is closed.
On Activate	To display a custom toolbar or maximize the report window when the report window becomes the active window.
On Deactivate	To hide a custom toolbar when the window loses focus and before the Close event.
On No Data	To cancel previewing or printing of a blank report when the underlying query has been run with no records returned.
On Page	To draw a border around a report page that has been formatted for printing before it is printed.
On Error	To display a custom error message when there is a run-time error generated by the database engine.

How to Cancel Printing of a Blank Report

Procedure Reference: Build and Run a Macro to Cancel a Report That Contains No Records

To build and run a macro to cancel a report that contains no records:

1. Open the report in Design view.
2. From the On No Data event property, click the Build button.
3. Open the Macro Builder window.
4. In the first row of the Action column, select MsgBox from the drop-down list and set your arguments.
5. In the second row of the Action column, select the CancelEvent action.
6. Save and close the macro.
7. Open the blank report and observe the message box triggered by the macro being displayed.
8. Save the report.

ACTIVITY 5-3

Cancelling the Printing of a Blank Report

Data Files:

Cancel.accdb

Before You Begin:

From the C:\0848893Data\Making Reports More Effective folder, open the Cancel.accdb file.

Scenario:

You are pleased with the report you created for the Customer Service group, which enables the Customer Service staff to print reports for specific customers within a time period of their choice. There may be times when there are no customer orders for the specific time period, and you do not want these reports to be printed when you bulk print reports. You want to avoid printing in such instances.

What You Do	How You Do It
1. **Preview the rptCustomerOrders report for different time periods.**	a. **Preview the rptCustomerOrders report.**
	b. Notice that the report does not open, but displays the Enter Parameter Value dialog box.
	c. In the Enter A Customer Name text box, **type *The Happy Camper* and click OK.**
	d. In the Enter A Start Date text box, **type *3/1/01* and click OK.**
	e. In the Enter An End Date text box, **type *3/6/01* and click OK.**
	f. **Review the content of the report and close it when finished.**
	g. **Open the report again for *The Happy Camper*** with a start date of *6/1/01* and an end date of *6/6/01*.

h.   Notice that the report contains no data.

i.   **Switch to Design view.**

2.   **Create a macro and set arguments** to cancel printing.

a.   On the Design contextual tab, in the Tools group, **click Property Sheet** to view the Property Sheet pane.

b.   In the Property sheet pane, **select the Event tab and click the Build button for the On No Data event** to view the Choose Builder dialog box.

c.   Notice that the Macro Builder is selected by default. **Click OK** to open the Macro Builder.

d.   In the first row of the Action column, **select the MsgBox action**.

e.   In the Action Arguments pane, **set the following arguments**:

•   Message: No orders during the period specified

•   Type: Information

•   Title: LonePineSales

Message	No orders during the period specified
Beep	Yes
Type	Information
Title	LonePineSales

f.   In the Action column, in the second row, **select the CancelEvent action**.

g.   **Save the macro as *mcrMyNoData* and close it.**

h.   In the Microsoft Office Access message box, **click Yes**.

i. If necessary, in the Property Sheet pane, from the On No Data drop-down list, **select mcrMyNoData**.

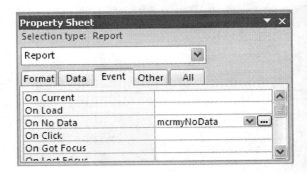

j. **Close the Property Sheet pane.**

3. **Test the macro.**

a. **Save and close the report.**

b. **Preview the rptCustomerOrders report and enter the following parameters:**
    -   CustomerName: The Happy Camper
    -   Start date: 6/1/01
    -   End date: 6/6/01

c. Notice that the message box is displayed to indicate that it is a blank report, and **click OK**.

d. **Close the database.**

TOPIC D
Create a Report Snapshot

You improved the visual appeal of your reports, and saved users' time by keeping them from printing blank reports. But, some of your colleagues might not have the Access application available to them, so you now need to consider how to expand the accessibility and reach of your reports. In this topic, you will distribute reports as a snapshot.

Printing and copying Access reports is the most common way of distributing the information they contain to many people. But, that can be time consuming and expensive and, unless you have a color printer and copier, the report may lose some of its visual impact. In this topic, you will learn a technique that enables you to distribute an Access report electronically to people who may not have or use Access. It also enables Access users to view a report without needing to open the database in which it resides.

Report Snapshots

A *report snapshot* is a file that contains an exact copy of an Access report—with all embedded objects—which can be sent to non-Access users. The snapshot will preserve all the objects, such as the two-dimensional layout and the graphics, contained within the report. A report snapshot file has a .snp extension. Even if you do not have Access installed, you can view a report snapshot, provided that Snapshot Viewer is installed on your system. The recipient of the report snapshot cannot add, delete, or make any other changes in the report.

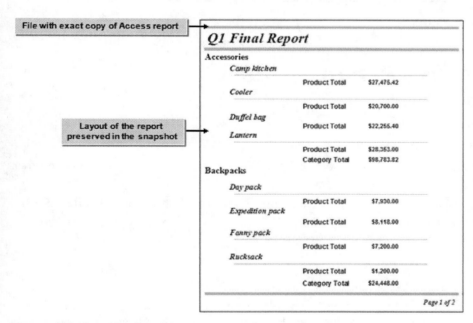

Figure 5-1: A report snapshot.

Snapshot Viewer

Snapshot Viewer is a simple program you can use to view and print an Access report snapshot. The program produces an image or an impression of an Access report. Snapshot Viewer allows you to distribute your report exactly as you had created it to others who do not have Access installed on their computers.

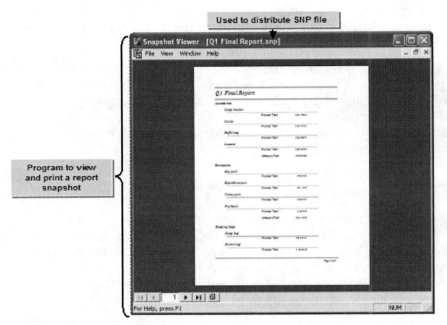

Figure 5-2: Snapshot Viewer.

How to Create a Report Snapshot

Procedure Reference: Create a Report Snapshot

To create a report snapshot:

1. In the Database window, select the report.
2. On the External Data tab, in the Export group, click the More button to view a drop-down list and select Snapshot Viewer.
3. In the Export-Snapshot Viewer wizard, check the Open The Destination File After The Export Operation Is Complete check box.
4. Navigate to the storage location for the snapshot.
5. Type a name for the snapshot file.
6. Check the Save Export Steps check box and click Save Export.
7. Notice that the Export-Snapshot Viewer Wizard appears again to allow you to save the export steps so that you can repeat the operation without using the wizard. You can retrieve the file, in case you had not saved it, by clicking the Saved Exports button on the External Data tab in the Export group.
8. In the Export-Snapshot Viewer Wizard, check the Save Export Steps check box.
9. Click Save Export to close the wizard.
10. Close the database.

ACTIVITY 5-4

Creating a Snapshot

Data Files:

Snapshot.accdb

Before You Begin:

1. You must install the Snapshot Viewer program on your system to view the report snapshot. You can download Snapshot Viewer for Access from the Microsoft website.

2. From the C:\084889Data\Making Reports More Effective folder, open the Snapshot.accdb file.

Scenario:

The president of your company has asked you to distribute the final sales report for the first quarter to all employees, but not all employees are Access users. So, you decide to try creating a report snapshot that you can embed into or attach to an email with instructions on downloading Snapshot Viewer.

What You Do	How You Do It
1. **Create and save a snapshot as Q1 Final Report.**	a. **Preview both pages of rptQ1Final and close the report.**
	b. On the External Data tab, in the Export group, **click More** to view a drop-down list, and **select Snapshot Viewer** to view the Export-Snapshot Viewer Wizard.
	c. In the Export-Snapshot Viewer Wizard, **check the Open The Destination File After The Export Operation Is Complete check box.**
	d. **Click Browse.**
	e. **Navigate to the C:\084889Data\Making Reports More Effective folder** to select the destination for the data you want to export.
	f. In the File Save dialog box, in the File Name text box, **type Q1 Final Report**
	g. In the Save As Type text box, **verify that the file type is Snapshot Format and click Save.**
	h. In the Export-Snapshot Viewer Wizard, **click OK** to run the wizard.

2. **Preview the report snapshot.**

a. **Preview both the pages of the report snapshot and close it.**

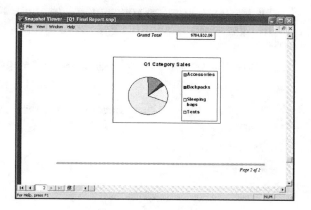

b. Notice that the Export-Snapshot Viewer Wizard appears again to allow you to save the export steps.

c. **Check the Save Export Steps check box.**

d. **Click Save Export** to save the export steps.

e. **Close the database.**

Lesson 5 Follow-up

In this lesson, you made your reports more effective. Since reports are your main way of communicating database information with others, it is important that they be as effective as possible.

1. **How will you improve your existing reports?**

2. **Can you think of any existing database that could benefit from the use of columns? Explain.**

6 Maintaining an Access Database

Lesson Time: 40 minutes

Lesson Objectives:

In this lesson, you will maintain your database using tools provided by Microsoft® Office Access™ 2007.

You will:

- Link tables between Access databases and reset table links using the Linked Table Manager.

- Manage an Access database by using the specialized management tools provided.

- Use Object Dependency to determine interdependency of Access objects.

- Document a database using the Database Documenter tool.

- Analyze the performance of the database by using the Analyze Performance option.

Introduction

Until now, you spent a majority of your time developing and customizing your database. After the database is built, much of that time will switch to maintenance. Database maintenance involves a new set of tools provided by Access. In this lesson, you will use some of these tools to maintain an Access database.

A database is a growing, changing file that requires attention throughout its life span. Access provides a number of tools that help keep your database performing optimally. Once you learn how to use them, database maintenance will be fast and simple.

TOPIC A
Link Tables to External Data Sources

You customized forms and reports using various Access tools, increasing their effectiveness. However, it is often not enough to make optimum use of your own database. You may need to link tables in a database to external data sources in order to provide the most recent information to those tables. In this topic, you will link tables to external data sources.

If you look at any business, you will find that many data functions overlap from one department to another. This can cause problems that range from conflicting information to outright errors in data. Linking tables to external data sources can solve this problem by eliminating duplicate data, reducing network load, and keeping everyone up to date.

External Data Sources

External data sources broadly refer to databases that have sources that lie beyond or outside the database in which you are currently working. It is not an intrinsic or an inherent part of a currently operating database. By creating a linked table, Access links a database to an external data source. The external data sources that can be linked to an Access database are data in another Access database, data in a Microsoft® Office Excel® file; data in a SharePoint® list; and data in a delimited or fixed-width text file, an ODBC database, an HTML document, an Outlook folder, a dBASE file, and a Paradox file.

File Links

File links allow you to create a connection between your database and a file to display information from that file in your database. When linking a file, the link is dynamic and any changes that are made to a file will automatically be reflected in your Access database. Creating file links will allow you to work with the data in a separate file without actually importing it. A linked table appears in the Navigation pane with an arrow to the left of the name.

Links Between Data Sources and Access

In external data sources, such as Access databases, ODBC databases, HTML documents, Outlook folders, dBASE files, and Paradox files, the changes made to a file are reflected in your Access database and vice versa. However, an Excel file cannot be altered from within your Access database, and a text file does not allow any changes except the addition of new records.

The Linked Table Manager

The *Linked Table Manager* is an Access tool you can use when working with linked tables. Using the Linked Table Manager, you can refresh links of already linked tables. This is useful when the properties or field names of the original table have been altered or when there have been changes to the local computer. A linked table does not actually contain data, but it stores a copy of the original table's structure. Therefore, you can refresh the linked table to update modifications in the field properties of the original table. You can also use the Linked Table

Manager to update links of tables you have moved to another folder or drive. The Linked Table Manager window shows a list of all tables linked to the database. You can select the linked tables you want to update from the list. The Linked Table Manager displays the complete path to the linked table and also provides an option to select a new location for the linked table.

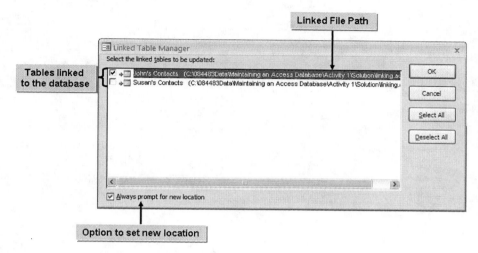

Figure 6-1: The Linked Table Manager.

How to Link Tables to External Data Sources

Procedure Reference: Link Tables to an Access Database

To link tables to an Access database:

1. Open the database where you want the linked table to be.

2. On the External Data tab, in the Import group, select Access.

3. In the Get External Data — Access Database dialog box, in the Specify The Source Of The Data section, click Browse and navigate to the desired location.

4. In the File Open dialog box, select a file and click Open.

5. In the Specify How And Where You Want To Store The Data In The Current Database section, select the Link To The Data Source By Creating A Linked Table option, and then click OK.

6. In the Link Tables dialog box, select the tables you want to link and click OK. The linked tables will now show in the new database.

7. Make a change in the linked table and verify that it is reflected in the external data source.

8. Open the Linked Table Manager dialog box.

   - Right-click the linked table you want to refresh in the Navigation pane. Choose the Linked Table Manager option from the drop-down menu.

   - Or, on the Database Tools tab, in the Database Tools group, click Linked Table Manager.

9. In the Linked Table Manager dialog box, select the linked tables to be updated and click OK.

10. Click OK to close the Linked Table Manager message box.

11. If necessary, save and close the database.

ACTIVITY 6-1

Linking a Table

Data Files:

Bob's Contacts.accdb, Linking.accdb

Before You Begin:

From the C:\084889Data\Maintaining An Access Database folder, open the Linking.accdb file.

Scenario:

Your company has just acquired a new sales representative, and you have been commissioned to add his client contact list to the central contact database. Since he is always updating his contact list, you do not want to keep reimporting his information. You would like to link this information to an Access database.

What You Do	How You Do It
1. **Create a link from the linking database to the Bob's Contacts table in the Bob's Contacts database.**	a. On the External Data tab, in the Import group, **click Access** to launch the Get External Data — Access Database dialog box.
	b. In the Get External Data — Access Database dialog box, **click Browse, navigate to the C:\084889Data\ Maintaining An Access Database folder, and open the Bob's Contacts.accdb file.**
	c. **Select the Link To The Data Source By Creating A Linked Table option and click OK.**
	d. Notice that the Link Tables dialog box appears.
	e. In the Link Tables dialog box, **select the Bob's Contacts table and click OK.**
	f. Notice that the Tables tab displays the linked table Bob's Contacts with a small arrow to the left of the table icon.

2. **Change a field value in the Bob's Contacts database and examine the effect on the linking database.**

   a. **Open the Bob's Contacts table.**

   b. Observe the company name in the first record and **close the table.**

   c. From the C:\084889Data\Maintaining An Access Database folder, **open the Bob's Contacts.accdb file.**

   d. From the Bob's Contacts database, **open the Bob's Contacts table.**

   e. **Change the company name of the first record to *The Western Connection***

   f. **Close the table.**

   g. In the Linking.accdb database, **open the Bob's Contacts linked table.**

   h. Notice that the company name of the first record has been updated to "The Western Connection" because you have linked the tables.

   i. **Close the table.**

3. **Refresh the table links.**

   a. On the Database Tools tab, in the Database Tools group, **click Linked Table Manager.**

   b. In the Linked Table Manager dialog box, **check the Bob's Contacts check box and click OK.**

   c. In the Linked Table Manager message box, observe the message that states all linked tables were refreshed successfully and **click OK.**

   d. **Close the Linked Table Manager dialog box.**

   e. **Close all open databases.**

TOPIC B
Manage a Database

Having learned to link tables to external data sources, you will find an ever-increasing amount of information at your disposal. However, to make efficient use of the added resources, the need to manage the database becomes inevitable. In this topic, you will learn about some of the utility tools provided by Access to manage a database.

A huge and expensive piece of equipment in itself does not guarantee success to an organization. The equipment can be an asset if it is managed efficiently, perhaps by undertaking periodic repairs and other maintenance. Similarly, possessing a large database in itself does not guarantee the perpetual integrity of data. To ensure the optimal performance of a database, it is vital you utilize relevant Access options on a regular basis.

Database Management

Database management involves not only storing, modifying, and extracting information from a database, but also preventing data loss and maintaining the integrity of the data.

Option	Basic Function
Compact And Repair Database	Ensures maximum database performance by minimizing errors and file size.
Back Up Database	Prevents data loss by storing a substitute of the original database.
Database Properties	Describes details about a database that can be viewed or edited.

Database Backup

The *Back Up Database* option is used to store a backup copy of an original database to ensure prevention of data loss in case of damage or accidental deletion of the original database. The backup copy acts as a reserve or substitute of the original database. The Back Up Database option is different from a standard Copy option. This is because, unlike the Copy option, the Back Up Database option automatically opens the Save As dialog box, allowing you to save the backup copy in a new location. Moreover, it gives a unique file name to the backup copy each time a backup is performed.

The Compact And Repair Database Option

The *Compact And Repair Database* option is used to minimize errors and reduce file size, helping to ensure maximum database performance. Compacting a database is imperative because deleting data from Access files does not automatically reduce the file size. Moreover, the number of errors might increase with additions to the database. All this can lead to the file becoming fragmented and the inefficient use of disk space. The Compact And Repair Database option helps avoid problems related to database corruption and unpredictable file behavior.

How to Manage a Database

Procedure Reference: Set Database Properties

To set database properties:

1. Open the database for which you wish to set database properties.
2. From the Office button menu, choose Manage→Database Properties to populate a property and create a custom property.
3. In the File Name Properties dialog box, select the Summary tab to fill a property.
4. On the Summary tab, in the Author text box, type the name of the author.
5. Select the Custom tab to create a custom property.
    *   In the Name text box, select Project from the list.
    *   In the Type text box, verify that the Text data type is selected.
    *   In the Value box, type the desired value for the property.
    *   Click Add.

Procedure Reference: Compact and Repair a Database

To compact and repair a database:

1. Open the database you wish to compact.
2. View the size of the database.
    *   If necessary, use the File Name Properties dialog box to view the size of the database.
        *   In the File Name Properties dialog box, select the General tab.
        *   Notice the size of the database.
        *   Click OK to close the File Name Properties dialog box.
    *   Or, right-click the Start menu and choose Explore to navigate to the relevant folder containing the database. Choose View→Details to view file sizes.
3. Click the Office button and choose Manage. To the right of the pane, from the Manage This Database menu, choose Compact And Repair Database to compact the database.
4. To the right of the pane, from the Manage This Database menu, in Database Properties, on the General tab, note that the size of the database has reduced.

Procedure Reference: Back Up a Database

To back up a database:

1. Click the Office button and choose Manage→Back Up Database.
2. In the Save As dialog box, select the location for the backup and click Save to accept the default file name.

3.   Close the database.

Backup File Names

The file name format for a backup copy is the name of the database followed by the date on which the backup has been performed: *Actual Database name_YYYY_MM_DD*. If more than one backup is performed on the same day, the date is followed by increasing numbers for every subsequent backup. Thus, the file name for the second backup will be *Actual Database name_YYYY_MM_DD_(1)*, for the third backup it will be *Actual Database name_YYYY_MM_DD _(2)*, and so on.

ACTIVITY 6-2
Managing an Access Database

Data Files:

Compact.accdb

Before You Begin:

From the C:\084889Data\Maintaining an Access Database folder, open the Compact.accdb file.

Scenario:

You have finally finished all your work on a new database and are ready to hand it off to a coworker. However, before doing so, you want to clean up the database so that it will run as efficiently as possible, and you want to create a backup to recover data in case of any damage.

What You Do	How You Do It
1. Specify the author and the project details for the database.	a. In the Compact database, from the Office button menu, **choose Manage→ Database Properties** to view the Compact.accdb Properties dialog box.
	b. In the Compact.accdb Properties dialog box, on the Summary tab, in the Author text box, **type *John***
	c. **Select the Custom tab** to create a custom property.
	d. On the Custom tab, in the Name list, **select Project**.
	e. In the Type drop-down list, **verify that the Text data type is selected**.
	f. In the Value box, **type *Course***
	g. **Click Add** to set the database properties.
2. Compact and repair the Compact database.	a. In the Compact.accdb Properties dialog box, **select the General tab** to view the size of the Compact.accdb database.

b. Observe the size of the Compact.accdb database.

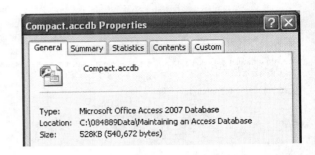

c. **Click OK** to close the dialog box.

d. From the Office button menu, **choose Manage→Compact And Repair Database.**

e. **Open the Database Properties dialog box.**

f. In the Compact.accdb Properties dialog box, observe the database size on the General tab and **click OK.**

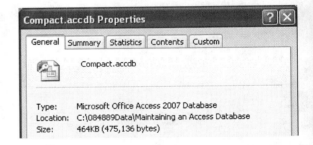

3. **Create a backup of the Compact database.**

a. From the Office button menu, **choose Manage→Back Up Database** to create a backup copy of the Compact.accdb database.

b. Observe the default backup file name and **click Save** to accept it.

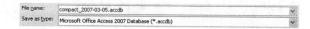

c. **Close the database.**

TOPIC C
Determine Object Dependency

You are now acquainted with some of the Access options you can use to manage a growing database. As you build a database, the tables and queries inside become intertwined and dependent on each other in order to function properly. Therefore, you need to determine the object dependency among Access objects before you make any changes that may inadvertently affect some other object. In this topic, you will determine object dependency using an Access tool.

A well-developed database can be compared to a well-architected maze. A variation in any one of the strands can enhance or ruin the beauty and design of the entire maze. Similarly, the Access objects in a database are interdependent. Understanding the relationships among all the pieces of a database can be very helpful when troubleshooting a problem. Determining object dependency will allow you to see the relationship between different segments of your database.

The Object Dependencies Task Pane

Object dependency implies dependence of a selected object on other objects in a database or vice versa. The *Object Dependencies task pane* allows you to examine the objects in your database and determine how they work with each other. Before moving or deleting an object, you should check the Object Dependencies task pane to see what other objects would be affected by the change. The Object Dependencies task pane displays two options for any selected object, such as Tables, Queries, Forms, or Reports. The first option helps to identify objects that depend on the selected Access object. The other option helps to identify objects on which the selected object depends.

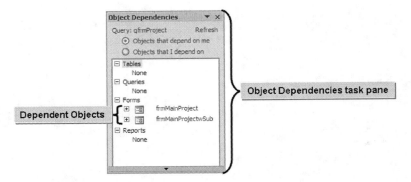

Figure 6-2: The Object Dependencies task pane.

How to Determine Object Dependency

Procedure Reference: Determine Object Dependency

To determine object dependency:

1. In the Navigation pane, select an Access object, such as a table, a query, a form, or a report whose object dependency you want to check.

2. On the Database Tools tab, in the Show/Hide group, click Object Dependency to view the Object Dependencies task pane.

3. By default, the Object Dependencies task pane will show objects that depend on the selected object. Select the Objects That I Depend On option in order to view the objects on which the selected object depends.

ACTIVITY 6-3
Determining Object Dependency

Data Files:

Object.accdb

Before You Begin:

From the C:\084889Data\Maintaining an Access Database folder, open the Object.accdb database.

Check the Track Name AutoCorrect Info check box:

1. From the Office button menu, click the Access Options button to open the Access Options dialog box.

2. In the Access Options dialog box, select the Current Database tab.

3. On the Current Database tab, in the Name AutoCorrect Options section, check the Track Name AutoCorrect Info check box. This is required for generating object dependencies.

4. In the Microsoft Access message box, click OK to accept that the option has to be left turned on.

5. Click OK to close the Access Options dialog box.

6. In the Microsoft Access message box that appears next, click OK to complete the process of activating the option.

7. Close the database and then reopen it.

Scenario:

Management has requested that you go through the company database and clean up any queries that are no longer useful. However, before you delete any query, you want to check and see if other portions of the database will be affected by its removal.

What You Do	How You Do It
1. Open the Object Dependencies task pane for the qryJunction query.	a. In the Navigation pane, **display the list of queries and select the qryJunction query**.
	b. On the Database Tools tab, in the Show/Hide group, **click Object Dependencies**.
2. Explore object dependencies for the qryJunction query.	a. **Verify that the Objects That Depend On Me option is selected by default**.

b. Notice that the frmViewAndAddContacts form is dependent on the qryJunction query, so deleting this query would cause the form to malfunction.

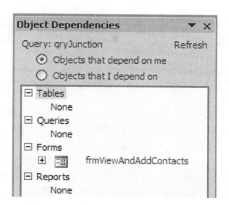

c. In the Object Dependencies task pane, **select the Objects That I Depend On option** to view the objects on which the selected object depends.

d. Notice that the qryJunction query draws information from the tblContact and tblProjCont tables.

e. **Close the Object Dependencies task pane**.

f. **Close the database.**

TOPIC D
Document a Database

You can now determine the interdependency of the objects in the database. You have realized that following this practice can prevent you from changing information in any object that could affect the functionality of some other object. As you work in a database, you might encounter problems that could have been solved if you had been more aware of your database's structure. In this topic, you will document a database using a tool provided for this purpose.

Though everything in a database you created makes perfect sense to you, others might not completely understand what your intentions are for certain areas. There may be times when someone else needs to maintain the database you have created. If there is no documentation for them to reference, they could run into problems. Having good documentation can help to alleviate most of this confusion. Browsing through the documentation of your database can help you maintain an Access database effectively.

Database Documenter

The *Database Documenter* option allows you to create a report about any or all of the objects in your database. You can control the level of detail that is reported by documenting only the objects that are important to you. This tool provides documentation with the design features of the database object. It reveals the properties, user permissions, or group permissions of the selected object. It also shows the relationships between the tables. Each object in the database is documented independently and the documentation is available in print preview and, therefore, can be printed easily. However, it is not possible to save the documentation report.

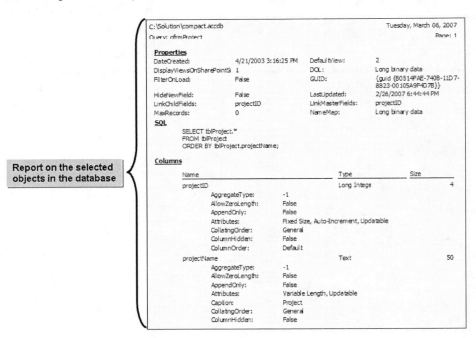

Figure 6-3: The Database Documenter.

How to Document a Database

Procedure Reference: Use the Database Documenter Tool

To use the Database Documenter tool:

1. Open the database you want to document.
2. On the Database Tools tab, in the Analyze group, click Database Documenter.
3. Select the objects for which you want to create documentation and click OK.
4. Review the documentation that is created.
5. If desired, print the created documentation.

ACTIVITY 6-4

Using the Database Documenter Tool

Data Files:

Documenter.accdb

Before You Begin:

From the C:\084889Data\Maintaining an Access Database folder, open the Documenter.accdb file.

Scenario:

Your company has just hired a new database administrator to help you manage the company database. Before the new hire arrives, you take the time to create documentation on the database so that the database administrator will have some reference material.

What You Do	How You Do It
1. Create documentation for the qfrmProject query using the Documenter dialog box.	a. On the Database Tools tab, in the Analyze group, **click Database Documenter**.
	b. Notice that the Documenter dialog box appears with separate tabs for different Access objects and a tab for All Object Types. Also, **select the Queries tab.**
	c. **Check the qfrmProject check box.**
	d. **Click OK** to create documentation.
2. Examine the documentation.	a. **Zoom in and page through the documentation** that describes the properties of the database object.
	b. If desired, **print the documentation.**
	c. **Click Close Print Preview.**
	d. **Close the database.**

TOPIC E
Analyze the Performance of a Database

You used the Database Documenter to identify the properties of your database, which can prevent confusion when object properties change. However, once a database is in use, you will also need to monitor its performance regularly to maintain the database effectively over time. In this topic, you will analyze the performance of a database using a tool provided for that task.

Monitoring the performance of a database will allow you to keep a close lookout for any problems that might occur. If you notice a sharp drop in performance, you can investigate further and potentially take care of the situation quickly before anyone even notices. Without this tool, you would not be aware of these issues until they were reported to you by a user.

Performance Analyzer

The *Analyze Performance* analyzes the performance of an Access database and recommends steps you can take to make improvements. It can be accessed in the Analyze group on the Database Tools tab. This option evaluates your database for efficiency. Selecting the objects to be analyzed in the Performance Analyzer dialog box runs the Analyzer and provides you with a list of analysis results you can use to improve database performance.

The Analysis Results list may include recommendations, suggestions, or ideas. Access performs recommendation or suggestion optimizations but not idea optimizations, which must be done by the user. However, a suggestion analysis result should be optimized only after verifying its consequences. The Analysis Notes section below the list displays information for a selected optimization in the Analysis Results list box.

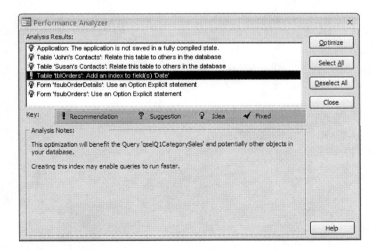

Figure 6-4: *The Performance Analyzer dialog box.*

How to Analyze the Performance of a Database

Procedure Reference: Analyze Database Performance

To analyze database performance:

1. Open the database you want to analyze.

2. On the Database Tools tab, in the Analyze group, click Analyze Performance.

3. In the Performance Analyzer dialog box, select the objects you want to analyze and click OK.

4. In the resultant Performance Analyzer dialog box, observe the analysis results in the form of ideas and suggestions.

5. Close the Performance Analyzer dialog box.

6. If necessary, implement the ideas and suggestions provided by the Performance Analyzer dialog box.

7. Close the database.

ACTIVITY 6-5

Analyzing the Performance of a Database

Data Files:

Performance.accdb

Before You Begin:

From the C:\084889Data\Maintaining an Access Database folder, open the Performance.accdb database.

Scenario:

One of your coworkers has asked you if you can take a look at her database and see if you can spot any ways to improve its performance. You do not want to waste your time by looking through every object in the database.

What You Do	How You Do It
1. **Open the Performance Analyzer dialog box.**	a. In the Performance database, **select the Database Tools tab**.
	b. In the Analyze group, **click Analyze Performance** to view the Performance Analyzer dialog box.

2. **Analyze the performance of all object types in the database.**

    a. In the Performance Analyzer dialog box, **select the All Object Types tab**.

    b. **Click Select All and click OK** to run the Analyzer.

    c. In the resultant Performance Analyzer dialog box, observe the ideas for changes to the data types of the fields, which will improve performance.

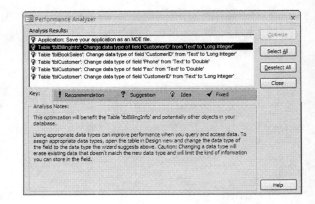

    d. **Click Close** to close the Performance Analyzer dialog box.

    e. **Close the database**.

Lesson 6 Follow-up

In this lesson, you maintained an Access database. Using the tools that Access provides, you can effectively manage your database over its entire life span.

1. **Are there any maintenance techniques that you have not been using that you will start using now? Explain.**

2. **What maintenance tools do you think will be most useful for your job? Why?**

Follow-up

In this course, you improved your existing databases by employing many new tools and techniques. You created complex Access databases by structuring existing data, writing advanced queries, working with macros, making effective use of forms and reports and also performing database maintenance. You are now able to turn your simple databases into robust, highly efficient databases.

1. **How do you use the advanced features of Access to avoid errors and rework in your database?**

2. **After taking this course, what things might you want to change about your existing databases?**

3. **What concepts were you unaware of before this course?**

What's Next?

Completing this course has prepared you to take the next course in this series, which is *Microsoft® Office Access™ 2007: Level 4.*

Lesson Labs

Due to classroom setup constraints, some labs cannot be keyed in sequence immediately following their associated lesson. Your instructor will tell you whether your labs can be practiced immediately following the lesson or whether they require separate setup from the main lesson content.

Lesson 1 Lab 1

Putting Existing Data into Correctly Designed Tables

Activity Time: 15 minutes

Data Files:

CompanyCentral.accdb

Before You Begin:

1. Open the CompanyCentral.accdb file from the C:\084889Data\Structuring Existing Data folder.
2. If necessary, click OK to ignore the error message.

Scenario:

The human resources manager at your company asks you to review a table in his CompanyCentral database that he has been using to keep track of employee data. From your initial review of the database, you find that you will need new tables for employees and health plans. You also want to make sure that you go back and clean up tables that are no longer used when you are done.

---

1. **Open the CompanyEmployees table** to check if there are any problems with its design.

2. **Close the table and run the Table Analyzer Wizard to the point to where the wizard has grouped the data into tables.**

3. The wizard has grouped the health-related data into table 2. The State field is out of place there. **Drag the State field back to table 1 between the City and Zip fields.**

4. **Rename table 1 as *tblEmployees* and table 2 as *tblHealthPlan*.**

5. **Complete the wizard. Review the results and then close the tables.**

6. **Delete the CompanyEmployees table from the database.**

7. In the tblEmployees table, **set Id as the primary key.**

8. **Create a table in Design view with two primary key fields: a five-character text field named Id and a two-character text field named HealthCode.**

9. **Save the table as *tblJunction*.**

---

10. **Close the CompanyCentral database.**

Lesson 2 Lab 1
Summarizing Data

Activity Time: 15 minutes

Data Files:

Musiccentral.accdb

Before You Begin:
Open the Musiccentral.accdb file from the C:\084889Data\Writing Advanced Queries folder.

Scenario:
You are working for a company that offers short courses on how to play musical instruments. In the Musiccentral database, you keep track of the courses offered and the students who have registered for the courses. Rather than seeing lengthy registration lists, you want to summarize data that is contained in these tables. For instance, you want to access the names of students who registered on a particular date. You want to view, in a single table, the names of students, their course type, and the number of courses for which they have registered. You would also like to create a PivotTable view of the StudentCourses query. This will enable you to look at the count of students in each class and manipulate the class codes and start dates to expand or confine the display.

1. In the Musiccentral database, **familiarize yourself with the design of qselStudentCourses.** This query combines data from four separate tables. **Close the query.**

2. **Create a subquery to retrieve names of students who registered on 4/01/01.**

3. **Start the Crosstab Query Wizard and base the new query on qselStudentCourses.**

4. **Designate the values in the StudentName field as row headings.**

5. **Select the values in the TypeCode field to be column headings.**

6. **Display a count of course codes for which students are registered as values.**

7. **Name the query** *qselStudentCourses_Crosstab.*

8. **Save the query and close the datasheet.**

9. **Open the qselStudentCourses query and create a PivotTable view with the following parameters:**
   - The TypeCode as a filter.
   - The StartDate as rows.
   - The CourseCode field as columns.
   - Designate the StudentID field as a Count calculation and hide the details in Pivot-Table view.

10. **Use the TypeCode drop-down list to confine the view to courses of a certain type.**

11. When you are done, **display all of the TypeCodes.**

12. **Close the window, saving changes to the layout. Close the database.**

Lesson 3 Lab 1

Creating Macros to Automate Tasks

Activity Time: 20 minutes

Data Files:

Healthcentral.accdb, Departmentcentral.accdb

Before You Begin:

Open the Healthcentral.accdb and Departmentcentral.accdb files from the C:\084889Data\ Macros folder.

Scenario:

The primary employee data in the Healthcentral.accdb and Departmentcentral.accdb databases is accessed through the Employee Data form. The employee data and the health plan information have to be accessed from two different forms, wasting time and effort. Also, when new employee data is being entered, the Dept field is often left blank, leading to records with incomplete data. You have been asked to address both these issues in the respective databases. You have to create a macro to open frmHealthData and attach it to a command button. The macro should also restrict the records using the Where condition:
`[HealthCode]=[Forms]![frmEmployeeData]![HealthCode]`

Also, you need to create a macro that will not allow the record to be saved to the table if the Dept field in the frmEmployee Data form is left blank, and it should prompt the user to fill in the field.

1. In the Healthcentral database, **create a macro that will open frmHealthData and restrict records using the Where condition.**

2. **Open the frmEmployeeData form and create a command button in the form.**

3. **Attach the macro to the command button.**

4. **Save the form, test the command button, and close the database.**

5. In the Departmentcentral.accdb database, **create a new macro that will make data entry mandatory for the Dept field in the form.**

6. **Add a macro action to the macro, to prompt the user when the Dept field is left blank.**

7. **Test the macro and close the database.**

Lesson 4 Lab 1

Enhancing a Form

Activity Time: 15 minutes

Data Files:

Bookcentral.accdb

Before You Begin:

Open the Bookcentral.accdb from the C:\084889Data\EffectiveForms folder.

Scenario:

The Bookcentral database stores information for the Canal House Books publishing company. You have been given the task of creating a form that sales representatives can fill out when a new customer places an order. It should include customer and billing information on the same page on different tabs. The form should also provide a summary of payments made by each customer against his or her order. The company has made a few requests:

- A Tab control to organize customer and billing information, where the customer information tab page has the customer ID, name, and contact information, and the billing information tab page contains the contact names, first order, and bill account fields.

- A calendar on the billing information tab page to assist with questions regarding billing cycles.

- A PivotTable to display a summary of payments made by customers on the customer information tab page.

1. In the Bookcentral database, **add a tab control to the frmCustomerInformation form.**

2. **Name the tab pages and organize the fields on the respective tab pages.**

3. **Create a new PivotTable form and add the appropriate fields to display a summary of each customer's first order by month and payment.**

4. **Save the form as frmOrderPayment and close it.**

5. In the frmCustomerInformation form, on the Customer Information tab page, **create a subform to hold the newly created PivotTable form.**

6. In the frmCustomerInformation form, on the Billing Information tab page, **add ActiveX Calendar Control 12.0.**

7. **Save as *frmmyCustomerInformation.***

8. **Test the tab pages, and observe the PivotTable form on the Customer Information tab page and the Calendar control on the Billing Information tab page.**

Lesson 5 Lab 1

Enhancing a Report

Activity Time: 10 minutes

Data Files:

Gourmetcentral.accdb

Before You Begin:

Open the Gourmetcentral.accdb file from the C:\084889Data\Making Reports More Effective folder.

Scenario:

Your boss wants to scrutinize the orders for each company sales rep. You have created a report that prints the details for the sales rep and month of your choice; however, sometimes an incorrect sales rep number is entered and the report detail is blank. In that event, you want to cancel the printing of the blank report by using a macro that you have created. In addition, you want to enhance the report by adding a chart as part of your printed output, to make the sales results for each rep more obvious. You want the chart to show the total for each sales rep, so you create a query to produce this data. Finally, you need to distribute this report to several coworkers, not all of whom use Access.

You have been provided with the following specifications in creating the chart in the report:

- Use a 3-D Column Chart.
- The chart should be laid out with Reps as the horizontal axis and Total Sales as the vertical axis.
- Choose not to have the chart change from record to record and do not include a legend.
- Assign the chart a title of Sales Rep Figures.

> In the Gourmetcentral database, rptSolutionCustomerOrders is a completed file of this activity. You can compare your results to this report.

1. In the Gourmetcentral database, **open rptCustomerOrders. Preview the report for sales rep 1 for the state of FL, and then switch to Design view.**

2.   **Insert the chart into the Report footer, basing the chart on the qtotRep query. Add the CustomerNum, Rep, and TotalSales fields and create a 3-D column chart with the given specifications. Save and close the report.**

3.   **Preview the report for sales rep 2 for the state of MN. Next, preview the report for sales rep 2 in the state of NY. After reviewing the content of the report, switch to Design view.**

4.   You have created and stored a macro, mcrNoData, which cancels printing when the report does not contain detail records. **Set the report's On No Data event property to this macro. Preview the report for sales rep 2 in the state of NY** to see if the macro works as intended.

5.   **Create a report snapshot for sales rep 1 for the state of FL, for which you had inserted a chart, and then view the report in Snapshot Viewer.**

6.   **Close the Gourmetcentral database.**

Lesson 6 Lab 1

Maintaining a Database

Activity Time: 10 minutes

Data Files:

Lonepinesales.accdb

Before You Begin:
Open the Lonepinesales.accdb file from the C:\084889Data\Maintaining an Access Database folder.

Scenario:
Now that you have completed work on the Lonepinesales.accdb database, you will be moving on to another project. Before your work is complete, there are a few final tasks the company has requested that you perform:

● Make the database file size as small as possible.

● Create a backup copy of the database in its current state.

● Check the dependency of an Access object.

● Create documentation for the entire database.

● Analyze the performance of all object types in the database.

---

1. **Run the Compact And Repair utility. Check the file size before and after the operation to view the decrease in size.**

---

2. **Create a backup copy of the database.** Use the default naming convention.

---

3. **Check the dependency of the tblorders table** to find the objects that depend on the table and the objects on which the table depends.

---

4. **Run the Database Documenter utility to create documentation for all objects of the database.**

---

5. **Run the Performance Analyzer utility and read the information given in the Analysis Notes box for each optimization.** Implementing the optimizations can help improve the performance of the database.

---

6. **Save and close the database.**

Solutions

Lesson 1

Activity 1-1

2. **What can be the major problems with the data caused by a poor table design in the LonePineSales table?**

   ✓ a) Customer names and categories are repeated.

   ✓ b) The table contains fields that have no related data.

   ✓ c) There are no primary key fields assigned.

   d) The Category and Product fields cannot be kept in one table.

6. **What is unusual about the design of foreign key fields in some tables?**

   ✓ a) The foreign key fields contain more than one value.

   b) The foreign key fields contain exactly one value.

   c) The foreign key fields do not form part of the table relationships.

   d) The foreign key fields are related to the primary keys of more than one table.

Activity 1-2

3. **True or False? Access was not able to append all the records to tblAssignments because the Append query contained duplicate records.**

   ✓ True

   ___ False

Activity 2-3

2. **What is the purpose of the calculated expression?**

   ✓ a) The expression creates a calculated field named Total Sales.

   ✓ b) The expression formats the result with the dollar sign ($).

   ✓ c) The expression totals the result for each group of products.

   d) The expression takes Quantity and Price from just one table.

Activity 2-4

7. **What features do you notice in the design created by the wizard?**

✓ a) The Crosstab Query Wizard created a totals query that also has a crosstab row.

✓ b) Each field is designated as Row Heading, Column Heading, or Value.

✓ c) The Date values are formatted as the three-letter abbreviation for the month and are grouped on that value.

d) The Crosstab Query Wizard does not sort the resultant data.

Activity 3-2

2. **When should the mcrMyContact macro be executed?**

a) When the form is closed.

✓ b) When the button is clicked.

c) When the form is clicked.

d) When the macro is double-clicked.

3. **To which event should the macro be attached?**

a) The Before Update event

b) The On Delete event

✓ c) The On Click event

d) The On Close event

Glossary

ActiveX controls

Software components that are modeled on the Microsoft Component Object Model (COM). ActiveX controls are usually graphical objects that do not operate as standalone solutions and run only in the Windows environment.

Analyze Performance

An option that analyzes the performance of an Access database and recommends steps you can take to make improvements.

Back Up Database option

An option that can be accessed by choosing the Manage option from the Office button menu. Making a backup copy ensures prevention of data loss in case of damage or accidental deletion of the original database.

chart

A graphical representation of information that depicts a relationship, often functional, between two sets of numbers or between a set of numbers and a set of categories, as a set of points having coordinates determined by the relationship.

Compact And Repair Database option

An option that can be accessed by choosing the Manage option from the Office button menu. The main purpose of this option is to minimize errors and reduce file size, thus ensuring maximum database performance.

crosstab query

A query that calculates and summarizes table data. Using the Crosstab Query Wizard, the user can choose the data that will be displayed for the row and column headings and the methods by which the intersecting data is calculated.

Database Documenter

An option that allows you to create a report about any or all of the objects in your database.

embedded macros

Macros that are a part of an event property.

external data sources

Refers to databases that have sources that lie beyond or outside the database in which you are currently working.

file links

Allow you to create a connection between your database and a separate file.

Find Duplicates Query Wizard

Finds records that have duplicate field values in a single table or query.

Find Unmatched Query Wizard
Finds records that are unique to one table or query, when two tables or queries are compared.

first normal form
A normal form that is used to design a table in which each cell has a single value and corresponds to its field name. Also referred to as 1NF.

foreign key
A field that is associated with the primary key of another table to which it shares a relationship.

functional dependency
The non-key fields are wholly dependent on the primary key.

junction table
A table that eliminates a many-to-many relationship between two other tables. The junction table's primary key will consist of both the foreign keys from the other tables, thereby eliminating duplicate records.

Linked Table Manager
An Access tool used to refresh links of already linked tables.

macro action
A self-contained instruction that can automate a specific task or a series of tasks.

macro condition
An expression that enables a macro to perform certain tasks only if a specific situation exists.

macro
A tool that performs a series of actions that automate a process or a set of tasks.

many-to-many relationship
An association between two Access tables where multiple records in one table can correspond to multiple records in the other table.

Object Dependencies Task pane
A pane that allows you to examine the objects in your database and determine how they work with each other.

object event
An action that is triggered by a user on a database object.

primary key
A field or combination of fields in a table that uniquely identifies each record in a table.

report snapshot
A file that contains an exact copy of an Access report—with all embedded objects—which can be sent to non-Access users.

second normal form
A normal form that is in the first normal form and is used to establish functional dependency in a table. Also referred to as 2NF.

Subform Wizard
A tool used to create a new subform in a main form or embed an already existing form in another form.

subform
A form that is inserted in another form that enables you to view data from more than one table or query in the same form.

subquery
A query that is nested inside another query. A subquery is used when the value needed by the outer query's condition is unknown.

Tab control
An Access control that allows you to create multiple pages in one form.

Table Analyzer Wizard
A tool that helps manage an existing Access database by suggesting how to make it run more efficiently.

third normal form
A normal form that is in the first normal form and second normal form and is used to establish a non transitive dependency. Also referred to as 3NF.

transitive dependency
Non-key fields are dependent on the primary key field or fields as well as some other non-key field or fields.

unmatched query

A query that compares two tables and displays the records that are unique to one table.

Where condition

A condition that filters and selects the records in reports or forms and their underlying tables or queries.

Index